HOW T...
ABOUT YO...

T

CLL

# HOW TO WRITE ABOUT YOURSELF

*A practical guide
to using your life experiences
in autobiography, articles, stories
and poetry*

Alison Chisholm
and
Brenda Courtie

a&b

First published in Great Britain in 1999 by
Allison & Busby Ltd
114 New Cavendish Street
London W1M 7FD

A catalogue record for this book is available from
the British Library.

ISBN 0 7490 0367 7

Typeset by DAG Publications Ltd, London
Printed and bound in Great Britain by
Biddles Ltd, Guildford and King's Lynn

# CONTENTS

# 1

# INTRODUCTION

Mention in passing that you are a writer, and someone will always say 'I could write a book – if I only had the time.'

The first part of that statement is true. We could all write a book if we wanted. The rider explains why many aspiring writers never try – few of us have time to put finger to keyboard. We have to make time, or steal it from some other activity. If we can steal sufficient, the dream can come true.

It is not enough, though, to have both the time and the inclination to write. There must be an absorbing subject burning within, an area in which we have special expertise. Writers are always urged to write about what they know. It is the easiest way to ensure accuracy. And what subject do you know better than anything else, better than anyone else? Your own life. The details of your life are packed away in the mind, and offer a rich source of material on which to draw.

Every life has the potential to be shared with succeeding generations of the family or with the world at large. Your story is unique, and this uniqueness endows it with a special beauty. Your story is one person's crusade, one person's adventures, one person's tale of striving and surviving.

## Some Reasons for Wanting to Write

If you want to write from your life's experience, some of your reasons for writing should be clarified before you start. Consider these thoughts:

● *Do you enjoy communicating?* Can you write a good letter to a friend? Do you like to chat for hours on the phone? If so, you are halfway towards writing about your life.

● *Do you want to preserve something of the essence of your being for people who will read about it when you have gone?* If you have published any material, then your writing can communicate with its readers after your death, and this end will be achieved. Writing about your life offers a form of immortality which cannot be gained in any other way. There is no need to feel silly or inhibited at the idea of reaching for immortality. It is a fundamental urge in each of us.

7

● *Do you want to make money?* This is not guaranteed, but you should be able to make at least a modest sum by writing from your life's experience. This will not necessarily arise from sales of your completed autobiography. Letters, articles and stories which are based on true events will bring in more money than larger projects in the short term. Speaking engagements, tutoring and seminars will also contribute, though you are more likely to be asked to give these if you have written a full-length book.

● *Do you want to leave information about yourself and your feelings for future generations of your family?* No matter how much or how little you publish, you would be leaving them a fascinating document. Remember, though, that this fascination tends to skip a generation before it begins to work its magic. Don't expect your children to be as enthusiastic as your grandchildren. And if you doubt that they would appreciate your material, just think how much you would enjoy reading about the life of your own grandparents or earlier ancestors.

● *Are you seeking fame or notoriety?* Publication of the details of exciting, extraordinary or shadowy events could attract more public attention than you anticipated. Would you be happy dealing with this? If you find the exposing of personal information intrusive, are you still willing to pursue your writing, knowing that intrusion might be inevitable?

● *Do you wish to describe some matter of general interest which you experienced firsthand?* This could be anything from working for a particular firm to being involved in a state occasion. The more general interest there is in your subject matter, the more prospective purchasers there are for your work.

● *Are you thinking about writing a book?* For most people, writing about your own life suggests a whole book, an autobiography, published by a known publishing house. But there are expanding opportunities nowadays offering other ways of sharing details of your life with other people. Magazines are publishing 'it happened to me' articles on all manner of subjects, from the heartwarming to the sensational. At the same time, the increasing use of technology in the printing industry and the proliferation of inexpensive desktop publishing packages have reduced publication costs. So it is becoming easier to find a mainstream or niche publisher willing to commission your autobiographical book, or for you to self-publish your own book.

If these thoughts have fired your imagination, it is time to start preparing yourself for the exhilarating task before you.

INTRODUCTION

## Preparing to Write

Once you have decided to write about your life, it is useful to devise a plan of action, and to establish the direction you wish your writing to take. Start with the inner preparation. Ask yourself:

● Am I enthusiastic about this venture?
● Am I willing to spend time and creative energy on it?
● Am I happy about the idea of sharing my experiences with my family and friends? Or with the world at large?
● Am I determined to explore all my memories, good and bad, knowing that I may be hurt when I relive some of them?

If the answer to all of these questions is a definite 'no', it's likely that you're not yet ready to start writing about yourself. Maybe you would feel more comfortable working on less intimate subjects for a while, but keeping your mind open to the idea of writing about your life at some stage in the future. After further writing experience, you might choose to cover more personal topics. You could, however, realise that you are never destined to write about your own life. If that is the case, don't worry. Nobody is forcing you to tell your story. But don't stop reading this book. It will show you how to bring an authentic 'feel' to your fiction, poetry, plays or whatever, because they are animated by the integrity of true experience.

If you have answered the questions with 'maybe', it is worth exploring the idea of writing about yourself more deeply. Perhaps you need to test the water by attempting a few sections of your autobiographical book, or by writing some shorter pieces about your life before embarking on the major work. You will find advice on writing shorter pieces in the first half of this book.

If you responded to two or more of the questions with a resounding 'yes', then you may prefer to launch straight into a full-length book. The second half of this book devotes itself to information on producing longer works.

Now start thinking about the more practical preparations you will have to make.

● Begin to keep a writer's notebook just for your life experience material. This may be chronological or random, covering a broad sweep of ideas or focused on individual facets.
● Do you have a good memory? If you have, recollections will come teeming on to the pages of your special notebook as soon as you start to

9

write. If you haven't, you might find it useful to concentrate on specific details. Set yourself a theme to explore. Try to recall one single occasion from childhood, such as your first day at school, the time you were given a pet, or how you broke your leg. You may surprise yourself with the quantity of information you have retained. If your memory still fails to provide anything relevant, seek out an old schoolfriend or have a long chat with your parents, aunts and uncles or siblings.

● Absorb the flavour of a particular time in your life by visiting the library to examine copies of the local paper published during your target time. (Back issues may be stored on microfiche or CD, but the staff will be able to help you.) While you're there, consult fiction and non-fiction books which touch on the areas in which you will be writing. Expose yourself to as much detail as you can of the times and places which were significant for you.

The next stage of preparation involves self-discipline. It is necessary to get into the writing habit if you are determined to produce finished pieces of work. No matter how much you enjoy writing – or enjoy the idea of being a writer – you will need to organise your life in a way that includes writing at its heart. For there is no point in writing if you're going to be half-hearted about it. Unless you are at least 105% involved in the task, you will not be able to enthral yourself as the producer of the writing or your readers as its consumers.

Be realistic about the time you have available for writing, and mindful of the comment that started this chapter – few people actually have time to write. Time has to be stolen from elsewhere. Examine your daily and weekly routine to identify periods of time which can be allocated to writing. Perhaps you have a free half-day in the week? Or maybe you could get up half an hour earlier or go to bed half an hour later, using the additional time for your writing? If you know you work well under pressure, could you take a 'chunk' of free time, such as a quiet weekend, and blitz the writing during that time?

If you're someone who works best with a deadline, try using the 'stick and carrot' approach. Promise yourself a simple treat such as a coffee break when you've completed two pages. Or deny yourself a walk or an hour with the TV if you have not achieved anything.

Keep your targets realistic. If you only have half an hour to work each day, don't expect to produce a chapter of your book by Thursday. If, on the other hand, you have six hours' writing time available, don't be satisfied with less than five hundred words.

It is probably best to see short pieces (such as brief features for magazines) as work to be completed at a single sitting. When writing longer works, think in terms of extracts, or fractions of chapters. There is always a risk that you will lose the spark of spontaneity when you leave a long piece of writing for a day or two. You may feel that you could never get back into the frame of mind from which your ideas emerged.

In view of this, it's a good idea to complete a section of a longer piece if you can and, if you can't, then at least scribble all your thoughts down at the first sitting, to avoid the break in continuity when a different 'voice' appears.

However you calculate your available time and the work achieved, it is essential that time spent writing is time you enjoy. Many writers are reluctant to get down to their work, but if they still feel reluctant at the end of a writing-session, then there is a problem. Enjoy your writing – and your readers will enjoy it, too.

## Keep It Light

It doesn't matter how fascinating the details of your life may be, few people want to sit back with a huge and dusty tome to learn everything about you in minute detail. Try to give your reader an easy read, which will offer entertainment as well as information. One way of doing this, if you're planning on writing a book, is to decide on just one aspect of your life, or one period in your life, and write about that. You run less risk of being boring if you don't feel you've got to include absolutely everything.

Everyone likes to be amused, and even the most serious events may have a lighter side to them. Everyone has come through life's ups and downs, just like you, and readers will sympathise with the downs so long as you remember to include the ups. No one's life is solid gloom and if you write a book that is altogether too serious, it will lack the ring of truth – because life's not like that.

A weighty autobiography looks, and is, daunting. Injecting humorous anecdotes and whimsical thoughts gives you a human face, and allows you to communicate a sense of pleasure to your reader.

If you were to go to a party wearing a morose expression and buttonholing the other guests to tell them your troubles, they would all try to avoid you. Similarly, if you produce a doom-laden book of sombre accounts and drab details of disaster, discerning readers will avoid you. Leave it to the retired generals and Prime Ministers to write their memoirs. Make your book a light autobiography – an easy read.

This doesn't mean your story should make light of its grimmer sections; but a narrator with a sense of humour and a desire to entertain will write with a leaven to lift the spirits of the reader. We all know people who, even in conversation, can turn a slight problem into a three-act tragedy, and we all have our favourite devices for quickly turning the conversation to more interesting areas. Those other people who can describe a serious problem with a touch of optimism, and who refuse to dwell on their difficulties, earn our sympathy. A book which conveys a determination not to wallow in self-pity is much more pleasant to read than one that whines at fate.

If you're unsure about this concept, read Deric Longden's *Diana's Story* (Corgi; 1990). The book alternates passages of pain and tension with laugh-aloud comedy, and attracts the empathy of the reader.

## Starting Small

If you find the prospect of writing a whole book fills you with dread, or if you're new to the craft of writing, then start with shorter items.

Readers' letters to the editor of a publication consist of a single nugget of information, recounted simply and informally. These give you the opportunity to try your hand at using information about your life. They involve the narration of a simple experience, told in a few words, or the quotation of some memorable or funny expression. They may be written 'soapbox-style', where you sound off about any topic which arouses strong feelings in you.

Articles allow you to examine an event or set of circumstances in greater depth. You can use a tiny section of your life experience to prompt you to write an informative article or a nostalgic piece. Select a moment of high drama or humour and expand on it. You may be surprised to realise how quickly the article presents itself.

Writers should always keep a copy of everything they send out of the house. If you are writing short pieces about your life, be sure to keep an extra copy in your 'life writing' file. Then, if you decide to go for the full autobiography, there will be several finished pieces which you can adapt for inclusion in the longer work. It's always easier to rewrite material you have written before than to face the blank page and start with something totally new.

If you're reticent about writing your own experiences, why not produce a fictionalised account? A short story may be supported by personal anecdotes, but they can be ascribed to a third party. The reader would not guess they were true.

Don't be too strict about sticking to the truth, though – fiction is NOT like real life. You don't even have to use complete anecdotes, which may be identifiable. Write a totally fictitious story, but set it in a workplace, holiday destination or city you know, and your personal knowledge will add colour to the piece. Create characters based on people you have encountered, and they are likely to be more rounded and real than characters which have arisen entirely from your imagination.

At an early stage, you will need to establish in your own mind just how heavily you wish to draw on the material of your life story. Don't cross the line when you feel you have taken personal references as far as they can go. If you continue writing when you are no longer comfortable with the words you're setting down, it's time to stop.

## Yourself and Others

When writing about your life, remember that while many references are personal, based on your feelings, perceptions and experience, a lot more will affect other people. As long as you report facts truthfully and don't libel anyone you can write about others with impunity. Some people are delighted to be included in your book. You may find, though, that friends and relatives are less than enthusiastic about being immortalised in your work.

There may be occasions when you are recounting events accurately, but their narration will harm the status or reputation of someone you know. Again, think carefully before you go ahead. The best autobiographical writing is truthful, but if the truth will hurt you might choose to omit or adjust details.

For the sake of harmonious relationships, you may decide to show pieces of writing to your nearest and dearest before publication. If you do this and they raise no objection, go ahead and publish without any anxiety. You may even discover additional information which you can use. Even the best of memories may be flawed, and discussing details with other people who recall them will help you to report on them accurately.

Remember, however, that people might object to being included, and if they do you should think carefully before your work appears in print. Flout their wishes and you may alienate them for ever. You will need to decide whether it is worth taking this risk for the sake of the particular piece you want to write.

## Quality Control

It is tempting to take a slightly self-indulgent approach to autobiographical writing. You are telling your own story in your own way, and you may see no reason why anyone else should comment on or criticise the work. But beware of letting through any writing which slips below the highest standard you can produce.

This is not such a risk when you're using fragments of your life for articles or readers' letters. If these are to be published, they will have to pass strict editorial scrutiny before they appear in print.

Whether you are preparing short or long extracts from your story, or producing a full-length book, make sure that you write to the best of your ability. A careful study of the information in this book will help you in this, as will a study of the work of other people who have written about their lives.

It is important to read widely in any genre in which you are trying to write. If you fail to do this, you will deprive yourself of seeing how other writers cope with the style of writing you are trying to achieve. While you read, pay attention to any areas of the piece which are specially effective, and consider exactly how the writer created that effect. Similarly, look at the areas which don't work for you. Decide why these are not effective, and you will have learned which techniques you should avoid in your own writing.

One facet of the craft of writing which is most important is the task of revision. You may have to rewrite your article or book half a dozen times before it conveys the information you're trying to get across to the reader in the best possible way. Revision is not the most exciting part of writing, but it's essential if you are to communicate with ease and clarity.

After you've produced a first draft of your piece, allow it to 'rest' for a while before returning to and revising it. Examine it as critically as you can, checking that the facts are correct, that the grammar, punctuation, syntax and writing style are appropriate, and that the information is conveyed in a highly readable manner.

Now put the work away again, and return to it after a few more days or weeks, repeating your initial checks. The best mss. (manuscripts) will captivate you – their writer – each time you look at them. If they don't, they are unlikely to appeal to their readers. This book will take you through all the steps towards your goal as you write about yourself, so that your writing is as good as it can be. Indeed, all the pointers in this introduction are expanded on in the chapters that follow.

Remember, if you are writing about yourself, you have a very important person as your subject. Make sure your work is a showcase for the most powerful writing you can produce, and you will be honouring your subject in an appropriate manner.

# 2

# GETTING STARTED

We've now established that your own life-history is a harvest store that can be drawn on for all kinds of writing, from the reader's letter or household hint to the full-blown autobiography. Your own experience of life can even be used to give dimension and credibility to works of fiction – long or short – and to poetry. As you read through this book, you will find there are chapters that will help you apply your life-story to all these types of writing.

You may already have decided which kind of writing you want to tackle, but whichever it is you will almost certainly find yourself mentally scanning your life's span so far and wondering, 'Where do I start?'

The answer is, 'Organise your material.'

## Organise Your Material

You may be able to dash off one or two short readers' letters based on fond memories of when the kids were young without too much effort, but once you get your material organised you'll find you have a huge cornucopia of memories and anecdotes to select from, write about and even, perhaps, be paid for.

And if you're hoping to embark on a full-length book, then getting your material organised before you start is an absolute necessity. Why? Because you will need to decide not just what to put in, but also what to leave out, and this is much easier if you've got an overall collection of memoirs and resources to choose from.

So whatever you're planning to write, it will pay you to get your material organised. What we're talking about here is gathering and filing – gathering together the many memories you have from all the stages of your life, and then sorting them into topic groups.

If you're a hoarder, you may find it easier to start with all your personal bits and pieces, all the letters, photographs, old programmes and newspaper cuttings that call to mind the many stages of your life. Let them suggest their own filing categories – childhood, school, war, national service, early career, whatever. But don't worry if you *don't* have boxes of memorabilia. What matters is the *memories*, and there are other ways of calling these to mind.

If you wish, you can set up a filing system for your personal souvenirs themselves, perhaps using shoeboxes labelled with the different categories. But what is more important is that you set up a filing system for your memories. After all, the souvenirs are just memory-joggers, and they're not the only memory-joggers you can use. We'll look at some others later in this chapter.

## Write It Down

The main thing is to make written notes of your memories so that they can be filed for later use. What do you remember? Write it down. What do you remember about the house where you were born? Write it down. About your school years? Write it down. Evacuation? Rationing? University? The swinging 'sixties? Write it down. Don't worry about grammar or spelling at this stage. This is your first draft, not your final polished product. We need plenty of material before we can start cutting, tailoring and finishing. The finishing process is dealt with in later chapters. For now, just write it down as it comes to you. Even a one-line note such as 'the day we went to Cannock Chase' is a useful resource in your notebook, because it will jog your memory later. So write it down.

Where do you write it down? That's a good question. Before you write anything down it's worth considering where the best place is to write it. If you're a certain age, you may still feel the pleasurable excitement of setting your pen to the first page of a brand-new exercise book. A small pocket- or handbag-sized notebook is handy for 'instant' notes 'on the hoof' (as we shall see later), but there is a problem with writing all your memories in an exercise book. As your book fills up you'll almost certainly find yourself recalling things that should really be linked to some notes you made earlier in the book. This problem can be overcome to some extent if you make clear headings that will be easy to find whenever you thumb through your exercise book looking for 'matching' material.

However, you may well find that loose pages are best. You can then keep them in their separate categories and add to them as more memories come to you. Write your notes in legible (to you, at least) handwriting on the pages of an A4 student pad or type them on A4 typing paper, then keep the different categories in separate folders. The thin card 'envelope file' type of folder is excellent, but used large brown envelopes would serve equally well. A single ring-binder with card separators will probably turn out to be too small for all your notes, and more than one will be cumbersome. If you're planning on writing a book, you will need a ring-binder for a later stage of your work (see Chapter 6), but for your full collection of gathered memories use your labelled envelope files.

If you're the sort of creative free spirit who likes to make notes on the backs of old letters, junk mail or Christmas cards, it might be better if you could keep those just for shopping lists and use standard student pads or typing paper for your life-story writing. For one thing, you will find it so much easier to sort, shuffle and select your memories if they are all neatly worded on matching pages. For another, whether or not you publish your writing, the loved ones who inherit your folders will bless you more for neat pages than they might for old till-tickets.

If you use a word-processor, it's easy to store your categories electronically as separate 'documents' or 'files'. But, even so, it's still advisable to keep paper copies too, because it's somehow easier to shuffle and make decisions if you can see all the written pages on the table in front of you. And often, the very act of leafing through the pages of written-up memories will bring other long-forgotten incidents or experiences to mind.

If you're gathering material from older relatives, you may want to use a tape-recorder. Certainly, making a sound recording of that person's reminiscences will bequeath a priceless treasure to future generations. Too many of us wish we had recorded all the tales our grandparents told us.

If you make sound recordings – or home videos – keep them safe, treasure them and enjoy them. But please, do also *write down* the memories shared. This way, you'll be able to sort them into categories and store them with your other memories in the appropriate folders.

## Memory-joggers

Some people are blessed with an almost supernatural power of recall. They can retrieve any section of their past life as if taking a video from a shelf and can play it through in their head, seeing again the exact shape of the flowers on the faded wallpaper, hearing the chanted words on the far side of the playground, feeling the dismay at the sight of a kitbag in the hall. Better even than any video, they can – at will – smell the steam that curled from the boiling copper in the wash-house.

Most of us have at least a few memories that are vivid and detailed like this. But to access the myriads of other long-forgotten memories stored in the locked filing-cabinets of our minds, we need to use memory-joggers. There are four kinds of memory-joggers that will help you: personal souvenirs, your own 'life list', shared recollections and documented history.

## Personal Souvenirs

Personal souvenirs we've already mentioned. A treasure trove of photographs, letters, cuttings, tickets, menus and the like will constantly and endlessly spark memories of times past. There's no pleasanter way of spending a rainy afternoon than browsing through these souvenirs and writing down the memories they recall. Write them on separate sheets of paper and file what you've written in the appropriate folders.

## Your Own 'Life List'

Some of the labels on your folders will have been suggested by your personal souvenirs, for example 'childhood', 'wartime' etc. But for a comprehensive filing system you may need to extend your collection of folders to include other topics on your own personal 'life list'.

A 'life list' is what its name suggests – a list of all the events and incidents that have been important in your life. You'll find this is a powerful memory-jogger. You could start by making a general list of life's natural phases:

>    Birth and baby years
>    Pre-school years
>    Junior school years
>    Senior school years
>    College or university
>    Jobs – in order
>    Early marriage years
>    Middle years
>    Later years
>    Retirement
>    Friends, leisure, hobbies

Of course, this list as it stands won't accurately reflect your life, so you will need to extend and adapt it into your own personal life list.

Don't forget to include topics that go right through life, like religion, festivals and holidays, house-moves, illness, bereavement. When you've got your own life list in front of you, make sure you've got enough folders for all your topics, labelled accordingly. Then go through your life list topic by topic, and jot down the people, the places and the events that were significant to you at that time. Spend some time thinking again about these people, places and events and you'll soon recall lots of memories associated with them. Write them down as briefly as you like, just noting enough to ensure you'll remember all you need to remember when you come to check your notes later. Then file them.

## Shared Recollections

Have you ever been at a gathering of family or friends, or at a special reunion, when someone recounts an incident from the past and everyone suddenly remembers? Then others add their particular memories of the same incident and your own 'forgotten' memories are similarly sparked into life and you find yourself recalling the past as if it were yesterday. Very often in such gatherings, you're surprised to find yourself recalling small details you thought you'd long since forgotten.

An unobtrusive tape-recorder would be a boon on these occasions, but it usually tends to inhibit the flow if people know it's switched on. And, so often, the best memory-sharing sessions happen spontaneously when you haven't got a tape-recorder set up and ready. You could, perhaps, always carry a pocket-sized dictaphone just in case. But those of us who are not so well organised have to make sure we write those shared memories down *as soon as possible*. Take a notebook to the lavatory if you must. It's so annoying to wake the next day and find you can only recall a half of what was said, at best. How satisfying to retrieve your notebook, check the jottings you made and transfer your 'written-up' memories to the appropriate envelope files.

## Documented History

One more memory-jogger that can be very profitable is documented history. The events, movements, fashions and technological advances that have affected our nation and our world over the span of your life-time have almost certainly had their effect on your own life.

War, the depression, other recessions, boom years; these events have all changed the way we have lived. So have changing attitudes – attitudes to war, to sex, to women, to children. Children once were seen and not heard, and a working woman who married had to leave her job. How did girls manage to emulate the long skirts of Dior's post-war 'new look' when their rationed clothing coupons didn't allow the purchase of a decent piece of fabric? Did you ever find a dry-cleaner who would tackle an embroidered hippy goatskin coat?

How did we travel before every family had a car? How did we communicate before every home had a telephone? How did we pass our evenings before the invasion of the television and home computer? What would your grandmother have thought of a dishwasher?

*Chronicle of the Twentieth Century* (Dorling Kindersley; 1997) is a marvellous tool for getting your mind back into past years. Its pages read like pages from today's newspaper and make past events and attitudes really come to life. Larger public libraries may also have an archive of local newspapers on microfiche.

Use your public library to research and recall the many changes you have lived through in your lifetime and the way they affected you personally. And don't forget to take your notebook!

## A Wonderful Resource

It won't be too long before you have a collection of labelled folders that are beginning to fatten as you add your loose pages. You now have a wonderful resource to dip into whenever you write about your life in whatever form. Don't ever stop adding memories to your folders. Every day brings its own experiences which, in time, will be memories, and you will still find yourself every now and then remembering something from the past that you thought you'd forgotten. Develop the habit of writing it down and filing it.

From time to time, go through your folders and write fuller versions of brief notes written in haste. Don't think of these fuller accounts as finished and polished and ready for publication. The reason for writing up brief notes into more detailed accounts is merely to make sure you have comprehensive and intelligible material to hand when you decide how to use your life experiences in your writing. The form they will finally take will depend on what kind of writing you decide to do – readers' letters, magazine articles, short stories, poetry, a book, a personal memoir just for the family, or the story of your family.

When you know what kind of piece you want to write, you will need to discover the best way to structure and polish your material for that particular type of writing. Many different kinds of writing are covered in other chapters in this book, including appropriate 'how-to' guidelines.

Once you decide what kind of piece you want to write, your question will no longer be, 'Where do I start?' but 'What shall I select?' How reassuring to be able to reach for your set of topic-labelled folders and dip inside for just the right anecdote or reminiscence. You will be so glad that you took the time to organise your material.

# 3

# READERS' LETTERS

If you are keeping a 'life' notebook as suggested in the first chapter of this book, or keeping a set of envelope files in the hope of writing a book one day, as suggested in Chapter 2, you will have collected a large store of material already. Reaching into your memories resurrects half-forgotten information about large and small incidents in your life. It also produces a series of cameos, 'one-liner' recollections which would appear as no more than an aside within a complete book.

These fragments can be turned into readers' letters and sold to a wide range of magazines. In this instance, publication is not your only aim. The cameos can be retained for injection at various points in a longer ms. to provide a change of tempo or a moment of humour.

Letters to the editor appear in most general/women's interest magazines and in local and national newspapers. Although papers are ideal for channelling requests for information, magazines are the outlets which would be likely to accept your cameos most frequently.

## Using Your Cameos

A reader's letter requires just one nugget of material, and although some publications feature letters of two hundred words or more, the majority prefer letters of up to a hundred words. This gives you no leeway to waffle, explain too much, drag the writing on after the punchline, or include any non-essential content. Practising the discipline of such taut writing is an excellent exercise for any writer. When you are writing from life, it is invaluable. It helps you to define and communicate the essence of your message without ever wasting a word.

To find the snippet of information the letter needs, trawl through all your accumulated notes to remind yourself of the minutiae of the events you were recalling. I was once making notes about a youth club camping holiday, and remembered the preparatory attempts at cooking on a campfire in the garden. The jottings merely pointed out that my attempts were disastrous, but the events which flooded my memories of that evening presented me with enough information to include in a letter. This eventually read:

'Before going to camp I built a fire in the garden to try some outdoor cooking. The sausages I fried smelled delicious, but clouds of smoke swirled in the pan. The bangers were hard and black, and when I managed to break through the skins, they were pink and raw inside. I was so indignant when my parents laughed at me that I offered the whole panful to the dog. He sniffed at them with a pained expression and walked away. Determined not to lose face, I ate the lot myself; and suffered indigestion long into the night.'

The anecdote contained around a hundred words"–"a good length for a letter"but needed something extra to catch the imagination of the reader. I simply added:

'I wonder whether other readers have had to suffer to save face?'

The letter was published in a women's magazine; and the rider elicited replies from other readers. As well as condensing the simple anecdote into a short, cameo form, I had been instrumental in providing a specific outlet for fellow writers who happened to read the piece.

This letter was based on a personal reminiscence, but the whole family can get in on the act. In fact, family get-togethers are useful sources of ideas. For one thing, they provide an opportunity for everyone to describe some event in which they have all participated, but which evokes different memories for each. They also offer an arena in which anything can happen, demonstrated in this (true) letter:

'My sister and I were staying with our parents on St. Valentine's Day when a sumptuous bouquet of flowers was delivered. It bore the address, but no name. I asked my husband whether he had sent them for me, and Mum and my sister did likewise. All three men agreed that they had sent the flowers, and we assumed it was an unexpectedly thoughtful conspiracy. A week later, the next door neighbour was complaining that her usual 'surprise' bouquet had not arrived that year. Quick wits, or wicked opportunism on the part of our "heroes"?'

Like the previous example, this is no more than a mildly amusing anecdote, but this too was published by a women's magazine. The fact that an editor thought the pieces appropriate for publication gave me confidence to store the ideas away for inclusion in a longer piece of writing.

Another rich source is the younger end of the family. Funny things that your children have said or done may amuse other people as much as they did you. If there are no young children in your immediate family, look a little further afield to nephews, cousins etc. A friend's daughter brought a schoolbook home to show her parents who read:

'History is about very old things like your Mum and Dad and dinosaurs.'

That tiny one-liner raised a smile on a letters page – and was later incorporated in a longer piece to lighten the description of a tense situation.

Each of these examples emerged from longer chunks of information in the 'life' notebook, but they could have worked equally well the other way round. That is to say, recalling light-hearted memories specifically for use as readers' letters will provide you with material for your longer work, just as the notes for longer work have been seen to prompt readers' letters.

These anecdotal examples are part of the story of your life, and when you are writing a longer ms. they can be woven into the fabric of your text.

There are also practical ideas which can fuel letters without relying on the narration of events.

## Household Hints

Many letter pages request tips, snippets of advice about how to make life easier or to save time or money. Probably without realising it, you have accumulated a store of tips over the years. They can relate to domestic matters, DIY, gardening, etc.

To produce a tip, all you have to do is make a point of 'watching' yourself while you perform some simple task. If you find there is anything you do to make life easier, then that is a tip for a letters page.

I have written – and been paid for – tips describing the addition of milk to pastry to improve its flavour; putting candles in the freezer for half an hour before lighting them, to make them last longer; the value of listing items taken on holiday and not used, so they may be left at home the following year; the keeping of a disposable camera in the car, so that one is never caught without a camera, and so that a picture exonerating you can be taken if an accident should occur.

You may be wondering what all this has to do with writing about your life. The answer is simple. Your own life's experience provided the material to be used in the tip. This experience may not be destined to become a part of your longer work, but it can have another useful function. If you choose to self-publish a longer ms., it will help to finance the venture.

Many full-length autobiographies are self-published, and you will read more about this in the final chapter of this book. A self-published autobiography can – and should – be funded by material you have produced out of your life's experience. Tips, anecdotes and other readers' letters are grist to the mill. You will be surprised to note how much money they can raise as long as the money is set aside in order to fund the major project. Sums of a few pounds may be lost if dropped into the general housekeeping pool. Keep them in a separate account, and see how they mount up.

## Opinion Pieces

Your background, culture, beliefs and experience colour the opinions you have on personal, social and political issues. They condition your reactions to anything you hear, see or read. Expressing an opinion in a reader's letter helps you to clarify your own thinking on the subject, to order your thoughts. Never feel embarrassed about holding your own opinions and writing about them for publication. They are as much a part of you as your physical appearance, and mentioning them in print helps you to build the self-confidence you require to write honestly about your life.

If you read a passage in a magazine and feel strongly about it – either agreeing or disagreeing with the line taken in the text – you can write to the letters page to express your feelings. Be sure to write succinctly and logically. You can approve or condemn the original piece as strongly as you wish, but be careful not to rant. If you can remain cool and collected in print, you will persuade other readers to your point of view far more easily than if you appear to lose control.

You may wish to respond to a news item in your letter. Be aware of its topicality. If it's a one-off piece of immediate concern, your response should be addressed to a newspaper which has a short lead-time (the time between submission and appearance in the publication). Magazines work a lot more slowly. It is unusual for a letter submitted to a magazine to appear within six weeks of submission. Three months is a more likely lead-time.

Some topics recur with monotonous regularity. The pros and cons of hunting, different methods of child-rearing, crime and punishment and the education system arise regularly, so you don't need to be too concerned about topicality in these areas. This means you can submit to magazines as well as to daily papers.

## Style

The style of writing you need to adopt for readers' letters is taut and spare, with never a wasted word. Draft your letter incorporating every detail of an event – and then check just how many words you can cut from it to tighten without losing impact.

For example, this is the first version of a true readers' letter narrating a simple anecdote:

'My friend came home from work one afternoon, feeling hot and sticky on a June day. She decided to have a shower and change her clothes. Before getting into the shower, she had to let her two labradors out into the garden. They went quite happily, and she stripped off all her clothes. The dogs suddenly started to bark, making a lot of noise which might have disturbed the neighbours; so my friend hurried downstairs and opened the front door a little, concealing herself behind the door as she called to the dogs. "Come in at once!" she shouted at them. But instead of the dogs, in walked the paperboy, whose presence had caused them to bark in the first place. My friend was very embarrassed – and so was the poor paperboy!'

This version might be true, but it is so longwinded that any humour in the situation melts away long before the reader has reached the end of the anecdote. (This account is far too drawn-out to refer to a 'punchline'.)

The next task is to remove every unwanted word, phrase or sentence from the piece, retaining a humorous angle. The revised version of the letter is:

'One sticky June day, my friend arrived home and let her dogs into the garden while she stripped off ready for a shower. The dogs started to bark noisily, so she ran downstairs and, concealing herself behind the front door, opened it a crack and called "Get in here at once!" The paperboy, who had caused the dogs to bark, appeared in her hall. I'm not sure who had the greater shock, but she never goes downstairs without a dressing gown nowadays.'

In this version, the tiny anecdote has been condensed to the essential material, and a punchline added. It sold to a women's magazine.

Whenever an anecdote refers to somebody other than oneself (as in the example above), it may be preferable to write in the first person"– writing it as if it had happened to you. Writing in the first person makes the incident sound authentic and immediate.

If you write a third-person anecdote (as if it happened to someone else), try to avoid using too many explanations. 'My brother's wife's second cousin's child' is complicated. A name, e.g. 'Bill' is not. You may feel that authenticity demands an explanation of the 'cast' of your letter. If you are happy stretching the actual truth for the sake of simplicity, do so. If you are unhappy, keep explanations to a minimum.

I remember recording a funny comment spoken by a child. The facts were these:

'A few years ago, our current church secretary's son (who would have been about five years old at the time) was explaining to my daughter, who was six, the significance of a country churchyard. He told her that when you became very old, they took you to church, took one of those great big stones and hit you on the head with it. Then they dropped you in a hole and put the stone on top.'

The letter which was published read:

'Graeme, five, had his own explanation for the gravestones in a country churchyard. Apparently, when you are old they take you to church, hit you on the head with a big stone, then drop you into a hole and put the stone on top.'

The situation is the same. The facts are the same. But the waffle surrounding them has been cut so that the nugget which fuels the letter is pared down to its essence.

Remember that the timescale of your story is unimportant. There is no need to mention that an incident occurred a week, a year or even ten years ago. I often recall funny things my children did and said, and submit them to letter pages as if they happened yesterday. (At the time of writing this, they are both in their twenties.)

The best readers' letters are informal, with the same chatty tone you would adopt if talking to a friend in the bar or putting the world to rights across the garden fence. Colloquialisms, abbreviations such as 'didn't' instead of 'did not' and the less formal grammar we use in conversation will give your letters an appropriate 'feel'.

Your simplest guide to understanding the style required by any publication is to study its letters page with care over a few issues of the magazine. You will be able to check that the content of your letter is appropriate for the page, and to note the tone of the wording of acceptable material. Naturally, the more magazines you study, the more easily you will be able to adopt the tone of a target publication.

If you decide to pursue letter-writing as a hobby, keep a dossier indicating the average number of letters appearing in a magazine, a random selection of the subjects used and any notes about preferred style (e.g. short sentence length, the use of first, second and third person, etc.).

## Submission

Whether or not you are intending to publish a complete autobiography, the letters you produce from your life experience will be intended for publication. You would be unlikely to write them unless you were planning to see them in print.

Readers' letters do not have to conform to the usual format for submitting mss. They don't require a covering letter, or a separate sheet bearing your name and address. They don't have to exhibit the conventions of presentation of business letters, with reference codes and the inclusion of the publication's address. You don't have to send a stamped, self-addressed envelope for a reply.

You can present a reader's letter as if you were writing a note to a friend. Put your address at the top of the page, and then begin 'Dear Editor'. Launch straight into your material without preamble. For example, you would not begin:

'Dear Editor
Here is a story about a funny thing that happened to me, submitted for your consideration. On our last holiday ... etc.'

You would simply say:

'Dear Editor
On our last holiday... etc.'

Letters should be typed or word-processed if possible, but you don't have to use the double spacing which appears on other mss. (as outlined in Chapter 10). Single spacing is adequate, while one-and-a-half spaces between lines is better. A4 paper is preferred, but smaller sheets may be used.

Readers' letters are the only mss. you may submit in handwriting. Remember, though, that you are trying to make life as easy as possible for the editor, so unless your writing is perfect and easy to read, use block capitals throughout.

Many letters pages will offer additional payment for relevant photographs, or even for a picture of yourself to print beside the letter. As long as a photograph is clear and has good definition, an ordinary colour print is acceptable in most cases. (Send the actual picture rather than the negative.)

Your name and address should appear on the back of the picture, but avoid writing on the photograph itself. Apply a sticky label or 'Post-it' note with the details to prevent damage to the picture, and in this case do be sure to send a stamped, addressed, stiffened envelope for its return. Stiffened envelopes may be bought, or you can simply put a piece of cardboard into your s.a.e. Some magazines state that they never return photos, so never send your only copy of a precious picture to these publications. In fact, as there is always the tiny chance that a picture could go astray even in the most efficient editorial office, it's a good idea to retain the negative or a copy of any photo you send.

It is also a good idea to keep a small supply of photographs available for publication. Invest in a film and have someone take 'posed' portrait pictures of you and also 'spontaneous' pictures to illustrate the anecdotes and tips you are intending to submit. (Order two sets of prints when the film is developed, as this is far more economical than ordering extra copies piecemeal when you need them.) Keeping a store of snapshots saves you from panicking when a letters page editor rings you up and asks for a picture by return of post.

## Keeping Records

When you delve into memories to retrieve your first anecdote for a reader's letter, you think you will never forget how it was worded and where it was sent. As soon as two or more letters have left your house, you are likely to forget which went where, and whether it was accepted.

You do not need a particularly sophisticated record-keeping system. Always take a copy of your letter, and jot its destination on the sheet. Store these copies in an envelope file, and you will be able to tell at a glance the destination and fate of each letter. If a letter is published, remove the copy from your file. If at least six months have passed and you've heard nothing, you can safely assume that the work has not been selected for publication.

Have another look at the copy of an 'unused' letter after the six months, and ask yourself if you could have done better. Be honest with the reply. If it is 'yes', re-work the material until you're completely satisfied with it. If it is 'no', check for other potential outlets for the idea/treatment and submit it elsewhere (again marking the destination and the new date on the copy).

You can continue this process indefinitely. So many magazines print letters of the styles suggested here that you can usually find someone, somewhere who wants to publish your letter.

Writing teaches patience. But don't sit passively by while you wait. Work on the next few readers' letters, and submit them at regular intervals to a range of magazines. Remember that no letter should be sent to two or more outlets simultaneously, and that you should be punctilious about letting the full six months elapse between submission of the same material, unless you are advised that the ms. will not be appearing in print.

The business of writing letters can become so absorbing that you may branch out to specialise in them. It also gives you the perfect 'testing ground' for cameo ideas.

Whenever you originate a letter, be sure to put an extra copy of it away in your 'life list'. The collection of anecdotal cameos will become a source you can dip into repeatedly to 'lift' the text of your longer work with a moment of light relief. The tips you have collected over the years could be grouped together into an article or even a non-fiction book.

## Additional Thoughts

Writing up tiny areas of your life experience in letter form will not get you widely noticed, nor will it bring in enough cash for you to give up the day job. However, there are some distinct advantages to producing these shorter pieces:

● It's a good idea to have a variety of writing endeavours out of your house at any given time. Feed plenty of pieces into the pipeline, and the end result could be a steady stream of acceptances. More importantly, the invigorating sense of being a writer is heightened if there's always a reason to look out for the postman.

● Each individual letter requires only a tiny slot of time for its completion. If you keep a note of all the ideas that come to you jotted in your 'life' notebook, you will have a plentiful supply of source material. Glance at the notebook, write the letter"and you will have taken only a few minutes from your store of free time.

● Use your letters as a 'warming-up' exercise before you launch into a long spell of work on your larger project. When you come to the project, your thought-processes and your fingers will fly as ideas and memories come tumbling forth.

● Remember to keep the money earned from these letters in a special fund, ensuring that you are building up a balance to go towards the cost of a self-publishing venture, expenses of travelling around to check records, or even the purchase of word-processing equipment.

● Always keep your mind open to memories and experiences which may pop a cameo into your head. When it comes, don't question it too much. Be grateful and record it. There is plenty of time for the inquisition afterwards, when you have harnessed the idea to paper so that it cannot escape your recall.

● When you use extracts from your 'life' notebook for readers' letters, you may find that you are sublimating the desire to put your thoughts and feelings on record. If you are happy with letters and have no desire to write lengthier pieces, so be it. If your appetite is whetted and you want to create something a little deeper, why not experiment with longer articles?

# 4

# ARTICLES

While the reader's letter takes no more than a sliver of your life's story, an article still concentrates on no more than one facet of it, but is longer and goes into greater depth. The term 'article' or 'feature' covers several styles of presentation. The writing may be nostalgic, humorous, confessional or informative/instructional (considered together in this context).

Like the reader's letter, the article has no space for waffle or flabby use of language, in spite of its additional wordage. If possible, it should entertain in addition to communicating its content. You are aiming to create an easy read, which means that you have to work hard on the article to make it sound spontaneous and natural. Sorry if that sounds like a contradiction in terms!

As Sheridan asserted:

'You write with ease, to show your breeding,
But easy writing's curst hard reading.'

It follows that the easiest read is 'curst hard' writing.

## Why Write Articles?

It is important to know why you are writing articles about your life before you launch into them. It may be because:

● You can order your thoughts more effectively if you're writing them down.
● You're intending to write a book about your life, and would like to produce a few articles first which may be slipped into the text with just a little alteration. Filling in the gaps between the already-written articles is less daunting than starting from nothing.
● You want to see whether an editor would be at all interested in your story.
● You want to create a market for a longer piece by tempting readers in with 'showcase' articles which will make them want more.
● You want the world to know about some injustice/fact/ emotion/sensational story you need to get off your chest.

35

● You relish the idea of being recognised as a writer through correspondence with editors, occasional acceptances – and even occasional rejections which still make us feel like 'real' writers.

Any of these spurs to writing – or any others you may be experiencing – should prompt you to write to the best of your ability for your target outlet. But it doesn't necessarily mean you can write exactly what you want and get it published. If you're writing for publication, you need to decide at the outset which target (magazine, newspaper etc.) you are aiming for, and then produce a piece which is totally compatible with their requirements. You are far more likely to get an acceptance when you work this way than if you produce the piece you're burning to write and then start shopping around for a market.

If you're writing just for the pleasure of your nearest and dearest, you owe them no less than the best you can accomplish, and you can write in your own preferred style and to any length without worrying about the restrictions of an outlet's requirements.

## Ordering Your Ideas

Before beginning to write an article, it's a good idea to make a list of all the notes you might choose to include. These may be taken from your 'life' notebook or directly from your memory. Jot down everything which might be relevant. Then, once you have established the angle your article will follow, you will have all the possible ingredients at your disposal. You will often find that the information contained in your article may be angled in different directions, and that you will, in fact, be able to produce a number of articles drawing on the same material.

There are various techniques for analysing a subject and considering angles of approach. My preferred method is to make a list of everything I can think of in relation to the theme. Then I use coloured highlighter pens to group points which seem to fit together and could be used in the same article. Some points overlap, and are marked with two or more colours. Remember that there is no copyright on facts, and so the same information may be used more than once. Naturally, you will be wording this factual information differently for each outlet, so there's no problem with including it in more than one piece.

Perhaps this note-making and grouping can be explained more easily with an example. One area of life experience on which I have drawn several times to produce articles is my work as a teacher of public speaking. A list of notes on this theme could include:

1  relaxation and breathing exercises
2  techniques of voice production, vowel and consonant sounds, clarity of articulation
3  basic speech exercises
4  constructing a speech
5  reminder notes versus written copy
6  public speaking examinations
7  your first public speech
8  self-publicity for the speaker
9  booking arrangements – venue, date, time, nature of speech required, fee and expenses
10 preparations on the day of the speech – clothes, accessories, books to sell
11 posture, stance, movement and gesture on the platform
12 using a microphone
13 reacting to audience response – changing the speech for the next group
14 reacting to audience response – changing the speech while you are on your feet
15 speaking disasters
16 funny things that happen when you go out speaking
17 return visits

I have numbered the notes here for ease of reference. The material could be divided up in this fashion:

| | |
|---|---|
| Technical article for public speaking students and teachers | 1, 2, 3, 4, 6 |
| Humorous anecdotal article about public speaking experiences | 15, 16 |
| Informative article for somebody making a single speech | 4, 5, 10, 11, 12 |
| Advice article for writers who are asked to speak | 4, 5, 7, 8, 9, 10,11,12,17 |
| Advanced advice article for experienced speakers | 8, 13, 14, 17 |
| Advice article for nervous speakers | 1, 2, 5, 6, 10, 11, 12 |

These are just a few suggestions. With a little lateral thinking, the same material could be written up for at least a dozen more articles.

You will see that some of the points appear in several content lists. Their angle would always be altered to suit the target readers. It is not a case of dropping stock paragraphs into every piece. The information must be moulded into a form which is relevant for the intended readers.

You will also note that some of the lists are considerably longer than others. Keep your mind open to the possibility of supplying an article in two parts. This allows you to treat every facet of the subject in sufficient detail – and doubles your fee.

At the beginning of this chapter I mentioned four general types of article. Let us now examine the requirements for each.

## Nostalgic Articles

These are features which refer back to past time. The term 'nostalgia' may evoke quaint, happy and distinctly rose-tinted days, but there is no reason why memories should be like this. In fact, memories of deprivation and misfortune are popular with readers – if only because they make them think 'Maybe my life isn't so bad after all.'

Don't try to produce an article about 'my childhood'. The remit is far too vague, and if you examined every facet of it you would be writing a book rather than an article. Focus instead on a particular area. Here are a few ideas:

● Earliest memories – which may be supplemented with things you have been told about your early childhood by relatives and friends.
● My first day at school. Try to recall it chronologically, or remember the name of your teacher and of the child who sat beside you. Were there traditional desks or informal tables? Did you use paints, crayons, pencils? Did you have to do any work, or did you play? How did you feel when you were first left in the classroom?
● Birthday parties. What did you wear? What games did you play? What was everyone's favourite food at teatime? What cards and gifts did you receive? Did anything go wrong?
● Illness. How were you treated for minor ailments? Can you remember any of your Gran's favourite remedies? Do you remember being taken to the doctor's surgery or to be seen by doctors and nurses in the hospital? How did they compare with today's health professionals? Did you have to stay in hospital? Again, how did it compare with today?
● Holidays. Did you ever go on holiday? Think about day trips; or about longer visits to relatives or to hotels/boarding houses/holiday

camps etc. What was the best part? What was the worst part? Have you ever tried to relive a childhood holiday?

● Family and friends. Did you live at home with two parents? With one? In a children's home or with foster parents? Did you have any siblings? Were there happy times? Jealousies? Arguments? Who was your best friend? How did you spend your time together? What was your favourite occupation in good weather? In poor weather? Did you ever do anything mischievous? Downright naughty? How were you punished?

● Food. Were your tastes different when you were a child? What do you eat now that you didn't have then? What did you eat then that you can't buy now? Do you remember picnics? What were your favourite sweets?

● Christmas. How did you celebrate? Did you have traditions that became a ritual every year? When and where did you open your presents? What was the most exciting gift you can remember? What was your least favourite? Who cooked Christmas dinner? Did you spend Christmas Day with the nuclear or extended family? With friends?

You will be able to add plenty more themes to the list, and although the suggestions all relate to childhood, topics for nostalgic articles include everything that has happened in the past, two, twenty-two or fifty-two years ago. Recall them as completely and honestly as you can, and you will have accrued the information you need to write a nostalgic article.

Perhaps the best way to approach this form of article is to make notes 'brainstorm' fashion about your chosen theme. Start by asking yourself a question (as indicated above) and then keep writing and writing without conscious thought until you have poured out in note-form everything you can think of. Write as quickly as you can, and don't look back at anything you've put down on paper. When you reach a sticking point, ask yourself another question and carry on writing.

When you are doing this, you may find yourself wandering from one subject area into another. Don't worry. Keep jotting down everything that comes into your head. Don't feel frustrated by this wandering into other areas. See it as a bonus. You are producing the notes for not just one but two or more articles.

Only when you feel you have exhausted the topic(s) look back at your notes. You might surprise yourself with the things you have recalled. It is a comparatively simple job to go through all the material and divide it into its distinct subject areas. (Again, highlighter pens in various colours may be useful.)

Remember, it is not 'cheating' to prompt your memories by checking details with your contemporaries. If you can substitute a chat with someone you knew at school for a session of making notes on your own, do so. The resulting information will be considerably more than the sum of the memories of each individual.

When you come to write up your material, try to avoid the dull opening 'When I was a boy things were very different ...' Launch straight into your memories without preamble. 'I found the dead frog when I felt in my pocket for the bus fare. I knew who was to blame, and there they were, sniggering from the back seat ...' has a lot more promise.

This style of article relies on a mixture of anecdotes and comment. Make sure you have at least four good anecdotes to relate. Select your best two stories, and use one at the start and the other at the end of your article. Just as you should open with a bang, so your final words should be funny/clever/strong enough to resonate in the mind of the reader.

Keep the style of writing conversational, and you'll make the reader feel as though the two of you are having a quiet chat. At all costs, avoid lecturing at your reader. You're sharing information with someone who is interested in your material – not hammering a message home.

You will find outlets for this sort of material in deliberately nostalgic magazines, county publications, women's/general interest magazines and also in local newspapers, but these may not pay for your article. Perhaps the readers who will enjoy this work the most, however, are the ones who comprise your most important target readership – your own friends and family.


## Humorous Articles

Bearing in mind that everyone loves to laugh, humorous articles are perennially popular. Humour is a matter of highly individual taste. The anecdote, witticism or aside that makes you fall off your chair laughing may leave the next person unmoved.

Attempting to please your entire readership will result in a bland piece of writing which ends up pleasing nobody. As it is impossible to appeal to everyone with everything you write, the best approach is to remain faithful to your own perception of humour. By the law of averages, it will appeal to some of your readers, and that is a bonus.

One of the principles of comedy is that there is laughter in misfortune, and this may be the richest source of humour when writing about your life. We can all tell a tale about a DIY, cookery, decorating or holiday disaster we have experienced. It may have been distinctly unfunny at the time, but it acquires the status of family mythology when viewed with hindsight. Start with the essential truth of a domestic disaster, and then embellish the tale a little to highlight the comic possibilities. Pile up a series of trivial calamities on top of each other. Add light-hearted asides and keep your best joke for the punchline. Remember that you can include relevant information which stems from a different occasion. You might write with truth about things which really happened, but they need not necessarily have happened to the same person in the same way on the same occasion.

As an example, I sold an article in this category to a women's magazine and to a local radio station. The simple fact was that I had to make a cake at the last minute for my daughter to give to a 'bake and buy' stall to raise money for her Brownie Guide company. The cake was a disaster, so I handed it over to the stallholder and then primed my husband to go and buy it back. When we got home, I found to my horror that he'd bought the wrong cake.

This story is not particularly funny or remarkable, but I pepped it up with some additional material. I described the mixing of the cake, and how in haste I had broken eggs directly into the food mixer instead of putting them into a cup first, and a quantity of shell was mixed in, giving the cake a strange gritty texture. (True.) I explained that while I was scooping the mix into a baking tin, I missed the tin and spooned half of it over the top of the cooker, having to scrape it off and back into the tin. (True, but it happened on another occasion.) I said the finished cake was burnt around the edges and still runny in the middle. (Always true. Anyone know how to cook a sponge?) I described how the cake had broken into three as I eased it from the tin to the cooling tray. (True, but that wasn't me. It happened to my Mum once when she had to make a cake in a hurry.)

I included a couple of general asides, such as the fact that I always did everything for my children at the last minute, as they never gave me notes from teachers until they were getting ready to go out, when they belatedly found them in uniform pockets. Hopefully this resonated with readers who had similar experiences.

I added spoof tips, such as when a cake falls apart, lemon curd glues it together more firmly than jam.

The final touch – purchasing the wrong cake – was described in some detail, relying on the 'just when things seem to be going right ...' ticket. I said how smugly content I felt, and how much I enjoyed the social evening knowing that the appalling cake was nestling in my bag. I ended the piece with an open apology to whoever actually bought my cake. (Genuine and heartfelt.)

None of these facts is funny on its own. The combination of them all and the manner in which they were told was designed to make people smile.

Tautness of writing is important in all forms. For humorous work it is vital. You will kill the comedy if you draw it out too long. (The article I've just described used about nine hundred words.)

One point about this sort of humour: it is funny when you poke fun at yourself or, in the gentlest way possible, at your family. It is just plain embarrassing when you poke fun at a third party.

Don't be afraid of going over familiar ground when writing humorous articles from your life – as long as you can offer some new slant. Humour may be politically incorrect, and there is still plenty of mileage in the fierce mother-in-law, mean Scotsman and similar old chestnuts, again as long as the stories have something original to offer.

Why not try subverting a hackneyed scenario for comic effect? The cliché of the strong male rendered helpless by a trivial ailment was given a twist in a piece I wrote when the male in question was feline. The familiar tale of the anxious guardian awaiting the return of a teenage tearaway was turned to describe my daughter anxiously pacing the floor watching for her grandmother's return after a dance.

If you're short of ideas for comic treatment, look at the material you used in any humorous readers' letters you produced. The slightest idea may send your imagination spinning along with your memories. You may find an anecdote on which you can enlarge without appearing to pad the piece artificially. Or maybe a combination of a few letters would provide you with an article. You might have half a dozen funny things a child has said or done. Each stands as a reader's letter, while, reworded and combined with appropriate linking material, the half-dozen pieces become components in an article.

Because it's so difficult to write humour with enough general appeal to make it acceptable, any writer who can do this has an outlet in a number of magazines and the 'social' pages of newspapers. And remember – humorous input is a welcome addition to your autobiographical book.

## Radio Talks

Both nostalgic and humorous articles have the potential to work on radio. There are few outlets for such pieces on national radio, but the good news is that they may be particularly popular with your local radio station. These are run for people in a specific area, so memories or anecdotes which are based in the listening area are of special interest.

If you think one of your articles might be appropriate for broadcasting, try it out. Read it aloud or record it, listening to gauge whether it would fascinate an audience. Read fairly slowly, aiming to speak at about 150 words a minute. Note any sentences which read awkwardly, or where the punctuation and/or grammar makes the piece difficult to say. Check that your sentences are not too long, and that they are not crammed with tongue-twisters. Try to avoid using too many 's' sounds close together. Their sibilance can whistle annoyingly.

Listen to the output of your local radio station to decide whether there's an existing outlet for the features you have in mind. If there is, contact the producer offering your work for broadcasting. If any interest is shown in your work, adopt the usual method of ms. presentation, with A4 sheets typed double-spaced on one side of the paper only (name and address clearly marked) and be sure to send a s.a.e. for a reply.

If no such outlet exists, why not suggest the inclusion of one? You could be doing a favour not just for yourself, but for a lot of other writers as well. Be prepared to read your work yourself if required, or to accept an actor's interpretation of it if this is the station's policy. You may not receive any payment at all, and if you do payment is unlikely to be generous. But your work will reach a local audience, and the broadcasting credit on your CV can only help with further submissions of your work.

Should there be no response from your local radio station, check whether the nearest hospital operates a radio service. These are often seeking original work, and again you will be gaining valuable experience, either in the art of broadcasting if you read the work yourself, or in the quality of your writing and improvements which could help it, if you listen carefully while somebody else reads your piece.

## Confessional Articles

If anything sensational has happened in your life, a range of women's magazines would be interested in your story. Just as good news is not news at all, a dramatic or traumatic true story is hot property. Stories of this nature involve ill-treatment, medical emergencies, crime, personal and domestic calamity, appalling problems at work and so on. Your story needs to be unique, or at least remarkable. 'How I failed my driving test' is neither sensational nor unique. But 'How I failed my driving test after the examiner had a heart attack in the car and I rushed him to hospital' has a lot more potential.

Look at the magazines that specialise in stories of this type, and then run a check through your own experiences to see whether any might fit the style of a chosen market. Note, too, the submission requirements. Some publications require you to write your ms. in the usual way. Others require only a thumbnail sketch of your story. They prefer to interview you in person or over the telephone, and then have one of their staff writers put the article together. This sounds inviting, and you may find there is a temptingly large fee on offer simply for telling your story.

Beware of a few drawbacks for contributors of sensational articles. A magazine may expect to use your real name and photographs. Is there anyone you would rather didn't know about your experience? Your partner, employer, parent, child and best friend may read the piece. So may your worst enemy.

Some magazines offer anonymity, changing names and using actors to pose for photographs. Would your details make you identifiable even if a pseudonym were used?

What are the legal implications of your story being told? Sometimes the most sensational stories cannot appear, for example if they happened to involve a crime which had not come to court. The writer risks being sued for libel if it is used.

What are the social implications of your story? Would you alienate everyone you know if it came out? How would you feel about the magazine contacting other people involved in your story to check facts? (This can and does happen.)

If you're perfectly comfortable about the exposure, go ahead with your confessional article. It could encompass an essential story you have to communicate. It offers you the chance to give the world your account of an event. If you are less comfortable, resist the temptation to tell all. The anxiety may not be worth the kudos.


## Informative/Instructional Articles

All the experiences of your life offer you the opportunity to inform or teach your readers. The traditional advice to 'write about what you know' can be put into practice in relation to anything you have ever done.

You might be surprised to realise just how much you have to offer under this heading. You might begin by making a list; but where the list technique described at the beginning of this chapter dealt with a single subject area in detail, this one has a much wider approach. It's a good idea to start by listing all your jobs, interests, activities ... the problem is not finding a subject to write about, but choosing which of a wealth of subjects you will tackle first. My own list, for example, might begin:

● Jobs. Saturday assistant in greengrocer's, bank clerk, speech, drama and public speaking tutor, writer, adult education lecturer.
● Hobbies. Swimming, theatre, reading, crosswords, writing, crochet, board games, visiting stately homes.
● Adult education courses studied. Silversmithing, human biology, make your own Christmas cards, painting, Italian.
● Life skills. Childcare, catcare, household management, car driving, typing.
● Attempted and failed utterly. Cooking, singing, knitting, novel writing, being tidy.

This list looks at just five areas. It could spread in many more directions, encompassing society memberships, holiday destinations visited, voluntary work, domestic maintenance attempted, subjects studied at school, failed hobbies, successes, mistakes made, practical skills ... any area of life in which you have taken an interest, casual or consuming.

Your list will contain some things you can write about in depth and with authority, and others in which you have a much slighter involvement and could only offer basic information. The depth is immaterial. Markets exist for writing based on all levels of experience.

With a little imagination and lateral thinking, your list will yield many and various ideas for informative/instructional articles. Here are just ten suggestions from the general topics listed above:

| SUBJECT | POTENTIAL OUTLET |
| --- | --- |
| 1 Basic typing exercises | Word processing beginners' magazine |
| 2 10 tips – caring for cut flowers | Women's interest magazine |
| 3 Balancing the household budget | Newlyweds' magazine |

| SUBJECT | POTENTIAL OUTLET |
|---|---|
| 4 Simple jewellery repairs | Handicrafts magazine |
| 5 Advice for new writers | Writers' magazine |
| 6 10 tips – painless children's parties | Parents' magazine |
| 7 Preparing for speech exams | Speech teachers' journal |
| 8 Advice for someone acquiring a cat | Animal magazine/local paper |
| 9 Rescuing cooking disasters | Women's magazine |
| 10 Devising your own board games | Children's comic |

These are all drawn from the brief list above and, as you see, they cover a range of areas. Ideas 1 and 4 show how just a little information may be expanded into a complete article. Idea 9 makes a virtue of one of the 'attempted and failed utterly' category. Ideas 8 and 10 could produce articles both for children and adults. 3 and 6 are based on a combination of experience and common sense, while 7 depends on a degree of in-depth technical knowledge.

When you consider that each of these ideas could be adapted to suit a number of markets, you'll see that their potential is vast. Include the possibility of merging ideas (for example, 'Bouquets on a budget' or 'Essential typing skills for new writers') to increase your scope.

An article of this nature needs to be structured with great care. If you're imparting information or offering instruction, a logical pattern through the material will make it easier for the reader to absorb the content. You will inspire reader-confidence if your information is presented in a controlled, ordered manner, showing that you know where you're going and how you're going to get there.

I find the best way to attain this pattern is to begin by making notes of all the points you wish to include. When you have jotted them all down, decide which note imparts the most important or most basic information. Number your notes in a sequence which allows the reader to accumulate a store of knowledge. Ensure that everything which should be known has been conveyed by the time you have reached your final note.

At this stage, I decide whether to present the material as a continuous piece with seamless links between the points, or as a numbered exercise. (You will see that two of the subjects listed above suggest a 'ten tips' approach.) If you're not sure which approach to choose, why not try both? For example, 'Advice for New Writers' could begin:

'Have you ever thought of writing for pleasure and, hopefully, for profit? The best way to start is by reading. Read books, newspapers, magazines, poems, plays – everything you can lay your hands on. Concentrate on the genre for which you would like to write.

'Start with a fairly short piece, such as a letter to the editor of a magazine or newspaper. Look at the other letters which appear there, and decide whether you have anything to offer which would be appropriate. You may prefer to make notes or draft a rough version of your letter first, and then revise and streamline your piece for submission ...'

The same material could be adapted to form a numbered points piece beginning like this:

'Have you ever thought of writing for pleasure and, hopefully, for profit? Here is an easy way to make a start:

1   Begin by reading books, newspapers, magazines, poems, and plays, concentrating on the genre which interests you the most.
2   Try a very short piece of writing, producing a letter to the editor. Look at a number of letter pages to see how other writers have achieved this.
3   Choose a topic which is relevant to a particular magazine or newspaper, and make brief notes about it.
4   Mould your notes into a letter, streamlining your ideas and refining the work ... and so on.'

As with all forms of writing, you need to read plenty of informative and instructive articles to ensure that you are familiar with the tone, depth, level and style required by different publications. And remember, the store of life experience on which you draw is not finite and limited. You have the potential to add fresh input to your source every day of your life.

# 5

# FICTION

The *Concise Oxford Dictionary* defines fiction as 'feigning, invention; thing feigned or imagined, invented statement or narrative; literature consisting of such narrative ...' So you may be wondering what a chapter concerning fiction is doing in a book on writing about yourself. The rest of this book does, indeed, deal with the writing of factual information, but a foray into fiction is a fascinating excursion, and invented material is animated and invigorated when it is reinforced by true experience.

## The Short Story – Ingredients

Consider the short story, the basic unit of fiction. As every story is controlled by its unique dynamics it is difficult to generalise, but a story comes into being when a list of ingredients is fused into a whole which has the power to grip the reader and insist on being read right to the end. These 'ingredients' are explored more fully in Chapter 8 to help you make your autobiography read like a well-written novel. Here, we see how some of the same ingredients are used by short story writers.

The list begins with character. A believable person with human attributes and frailties, interests and frustrations, joys and sorrows, and with whom the reader can identify is at the heart of most stories. (I say 'most' because the key character in a story could be an animal or an inanimate object.)

Characters will be more real and rounded if they are based on facets of people you know. This doesn't mean you have to make every detail about a character parallel with the person on whom that character is based. If you described the appearance, occupation, family circumstances and interesting habits of a villain to resemble a ghastly aunt or peculiar neighbour too closely, not only would you risk major upset, but you would find it impossible to give that character his/her head, to make the deeds and reactions recounted in the story compatible with the ideas you are trying to introduce. Real life would assert itself, and your characters would refuse to be themselves, but would turn back into the people on whom they were moulded.

It's better to incorporate a few traits from someone you know into a fictional character, or to construct a composite from a number of real people to animate your character. A quick and easy way to adapt a real person is to change the sex, rendering the character unidentifiable. Turn the ghastly aunt into a Chicago gangster or the peculiar neighbour into a woman of ill repute and their roots will not be recognised.

We meet the character at a moment of conflict in his/her life, a problem point. This may arise from the character him/herself, through relationships with friends, relatives or lovers, or via some outside agency. Problems from this last source would include an unexpected redundancy notice; injury when a car ploughs into a crowd of people; a misdirected letter which starts a strange chain of events. As the story progresses, the key character finds a way through the problem. This doesn't mean every problem has to be solved, but some hint of a route to resolution or the prospect of a way out of the problem makes an appropriate ending.

If characters are to live and breathe for the reader, they will have feelings, emotional reactions, and responses to everything the story throws at them. The content of a story must have some effect on the characters – or else there would be no need to tell it in the first place.

To give emotional depth to your characters, recall your own emotional reactions to circumstances in minute, and sometimes painful, detail. You may not have experienced the same events as your characters, but you have probably known elation, exhaustion, bereavement, despair, amazement etc. As long as the fuelling emotion itself is true and applied with absolute integrity, you can apply whatever events you like to the characters you create, and instil the proper reactions into them.

The story requires a backdrop and setting. Its content might unfold on a long walk in the Highlands, in the staff room of an inner-city secondary school, beside a hospital bed or in the cockpit of a plane on a stormy night. The whole story could take place in the same location, or there could be a number of 'scene changes'.

The setting of your story will have more authenticity if you write about a scenario you know. If you've never been to a football match, you're giving yourself a more difficult task than you need by staging your story in one. If you've worked all your life in an office, that's the logical environment in which to set a tale.

You don't have to pad your piece with descriptive detail. After all, since the advent of television, nobody needs to have an environment described inch by inch. The 'box' has transported us all into the rain forests, the courtroom, a luxury liner and the Australian outback. But the tiny crumbs of authentic information you feed into the story will satisfy the reader of your own knowledge of the scene. The reader will therefore approach every other facet of your story with greater confidence, being assured that you know where you are and what you are doing.

This is not to say that you should never use an environment with which you are unfamiliar; but if you do, make sure that the detail you inject into your writing is correct. If you are familiar with the environment, you can save yourself the trouble of research. You will automatically introduce the right information.

Most stories use dialogue to vary the tempo of their writing, and underpin the nature of the characters to establish them still more firmly in the reader's mind. Dialogue should be natural and unforced, as if it were being spoken spontaneously. It should never hold up the progress of the story, but aid its development. Each character should have a unique manner of speaking, so that the timbre which identifies a speaker via the voice will be present in the use of language within the dialogue. Some people speak grammatically, others in staccato bursts. Some make lapses of grammar in conversation, others interrupt or leave sentences unfinished. Characters may speak in a dialect – but this should be hinted at rather than hammered home. A northeasterner might use 'pet' as a term of endearment to a loved one, refer to children as 'bairns' and eat 'stottie cakes' for lunch. This places the character without the need to write all the dialogue phonetically, which would be tedious to read.

The best way to produce realistic dialogue is to listen to people talking. Writers have carte blanche to eavesdrop on every occasion, in order to research people's manner of speech for the sake of authenticity. Again, be prepared to draw on your friends for interesting expressions, unusual metaphors or similes, and pet words which come to life on the lips of your characters.

A good story starts at a moment of excitement, tension or drama. Stories which begin 'Sandra woke up. The sun was shining. It was going to be a lovely day' seldom hold the reader's attention as far as the second paragraph. 'Sandra woke up and stifled a scream. Surely that was the cabinet minister in bed beside her – or rather, his lifeless body' has a lot more potential.

The plot of your story – the things that happen – will be dictated by the outlet for which you are writing. If you are targeting a women's magazine which features relationship stories for the most part, don't have your plot hinging on the outcome of a sporting event. Bring your characters together, allowing their tale to unfold as you follow them through all its twists and turns.

There is no reason why your life experience should not supply you with a rich seam of plots. Everything that has happened to you first-hand, and everything you hear of secondhand (i.e. which has happened to people you know or friends of friends) is grist to the mill. Mingle genuine experiences with plots from your imagination, and you will have a formidable quantity of material about which to write.

Before you start to write, you need to have some idea of where your plot will lead. This gives you a fixed point on the horizon towards which you can begin to make your way. You may find that the plot changes direction many times during the writing process. If this happens, allow it to lead you down all sorts of by-ways. If the characters are sufficiently well drawn and their situation is believable, it is not surprising that some of them will want to take over. In fact, you may end up producing a very different story from the one you planned. That is a bonus. You still have the original idea to use another day in a different style.

The story does not have to retain a high pitch of excitement throughout, but there should be passages of light and shade, and a denouement which is believable and satisfying. Many stories follow the shape of a 'W'. They start at a high point of tension, let the reader down gently to a less frenetic point of the story, then reach a crisis. There is a second easing-off before a powerful conclusion.

Twist-ending stories are challenging to write and fun to read. In these, the reader is led to believe that a certain chain of events is building up towards an inexorable conclusion. In the last few sentences, the expected ending is turned on its head and something entirely different – but still compatible with the rest of the story – appears.

## Stretching the Imagination

The suggestions made above assume that you're writing about current characters experiencing the problems of today. Remember that, however things may change, people remain the same. Set your story back in ancient Egypt, or in Renaissance Europe, or in Britain during the First World War. The scene and surroundings will tax your imagination to the utmost, but the characters who populate your stories will experience the same sadness, triumph, love, rage and bitterness as you yourself have known. Only the external factors change. The inner ones remain the same.

Just as people in the past experienced the same feelings as we do, so people living in future time will – to the best of anyone's knowledge – know the same things. Use future time and as yet undreamed-of situations by all means; but if your story is populated by homo sapiens, the role models of today remain valid.

If you should choose to experiment with fantasy stories or science fiction, you may need to create a race which bears no resemblance to ourselves. Again, bring your imagination to bear, but make sure that the conflicts from which the story arises are credible for today's readership.

Should you be extending the length of your work, and producing a novel or novella, the information given for short stories remains relevant. In fact, in a longer work it is more useful than ever to base character, setting, plot and dialogue on people and situations you understand. You have to cover deeper, more detailed material with more profound conflict. You need all the help your life experience can offer.

Tales from your own life may be recalled as if you were watching them on a screen. The setting, characters and action fuse together in memory to provide a 'playback' facility in your head. They make an excellent foundation on which you can create drama, as you will be able to see the action even as you write it.

Whether you are interested in writing a play for radio, stage or television presentation, write with the germ of true experience in your mind and the characters will leap from your recall into your imagination and back, drawing on the finest resources of both.

## Truth into Fiction

If you decide to write a story, play or novel based entirely on your life experience, you need to know exactly how closely you will remain to the original. After all, if you're planning to produce a fictional story, it requires different dynamics from an autobiographical article.

Aim to develop the technique described for writing plays, where you encourage a series of events to dance across the screen of your memory in sequence. But beware of writing nothing but the bare facts. If you wish to create a fiction, you will need to use a degree of licence with the truth.

Be prepared to expand on the truth, embroidering here and there to introduce more exciting effects. Remember to omit the details of slow times when little happens. Tedious enough in a directly autobiographical piece, they would be the kiss of death for a work of fiction.

Make sure you understand the difference between 'showing' and 'telling' in your writing. When you show, you encourage the reader to identify with a character, and live out that person's experiences vicariously. When telling, you are – metaphorically – sitting the reader down and pouring a series of facts over him. This makes the relationship between reader and character too passive. Only the driest of copy relies on unremitting use of the 'tell' technique.

Remember that successful writers are avid readers. The best way to absorb the rhythms and style of fiction is to read plenty of fiction. Read all the fiction you can unearth for the sheer pleasure of reading it – then go back to the work you found most enjoyable. Read it more slowly and more critically, pointing out to yourself, even making notes about, the most effective devices that bring the stories to life. Then write with confidence, ensuring that your work boasts the same qualities you have admired in the work of others.

# 6

## YOUR AUTOBIOGRAPHY –
## STARTING ON YOUR BOOK

Just deciding that you're going to write a whole book about yourself can be a pretty breathtaking achievement – especially if your writing experience has extended no further than letters and holiday diaries and the like. But even if it's going to be an easy-read light autobiography, the real achievement is still to come and the actual task looms up in front of you like your personal Everest. How on earth are you going to tackle such a mammoth undertaking – write a whole book?

Please – don't panic! Whether your particular mountain is the story of your whole life or the story of just one part of it, your Everest can be conquered if you have a well-planned route and the right equipment. Without pressing the metaphor too far, this chapter and Chapters 7 and 8 will show you how to decide which path through your life your book will tackle and the best tools to use on your journey.

### Organising Your Memories for a Book

First things first: you need an easy way of gathering, storing and shuffling your writing. If you skipped Chapter 2, go back and check the advice there on organising your memories.

Some people find it hard to resist the temptation to buy a large bound hardback exercise book and write 'Chapter One' on the first page. It feels good, but this approach is not terribly practical. You're much more likely to produce an informative and entertaining book if you get your memories organised before you start the actual writing of specific chapters. There's nothing more frustrating than getting to the middle of chapter four and suddenly remembering a wonderful story that should have been part of chapter two.

So ditch the exercise book in favour of a set of labelled envelope files. Try to think in terms of building a collection of precious things, only these precious things are your memories – written down. And think of it as a neatly arranged, logically ordered collection. But please – *this collection is not your book*! This is your raw material from which you will *craft* your book. It will be a growing and changing collection, of course, which is why envelope files are more convenient than an exercise book.

Into your files go your various written-down memories, some quite detailed, others fairly brief and hazy. Don't worry about the vague memories. Once you start committing the clear memories to paper, you'll find that some of the vague memories will start coming into focus. Before you get as far as writing your book as such, you start by making notes and getting the memories that are in your head down on to paper and organised into a logical sequence.

As we've seen in Chapter 2, the titles on these sections could be the 'natural stages of life' listed on page 22.

early childhood
school years
embarking on a career
courtship and marriage
family life

You might also find it useful to include sections on the homes you have lived in, hobbies, holidays and leisure, friends. If you're thinking of writing about your time in a particular trade or profession, some section topics will cover all the important aspects of your occupation. And if you're planning to concentrate on just one particular time of your life, this will also suggest its own special topic headings. Whatever kind of autobiography you might have in mind, you'll often find that one memory sparks off another, and it's useful to jot down the briefest of notes under the appropriate heading and drop it in the right file. Then you can look it up later when you come to write the chapter where it fits best.

If you're already well into word-processing, you may be thinking that it's just as easy to store your notes in appropriately named files on your computer or word-processor. You're right, of course. Electronic storage is fast and easy. However, there are advantages in keeping hard copy pages. With handwritten or printed-out pages, it's much easier to compare one note with another, lay them side-by-side and perhaps shuffle pages from one section to another. And it's very encouraging to actually see your resource files growing fatter and fatter.

## Sifting and Selecting Memories for Your Book

So what will you select from your memories to go in your book? Well, not the whole of your life, that's for sure. It will be obvious to any writer embarking on a full-length autobiography that you're not going to write every single thing that has ever happened to you. Anyone who has written a holiday journal knows that a fortnight's experiences can easily fill a school exercise book. By that measure, the day-to-day details of a lifetime's experiences could fill several shelves of a library. A major part of your work as an autobiographer will be making decisions – deciding what to put in and *what to leave out.* Deciding what to put in to your book and what to leave out is like deciding which route to take up your mountain. If you get it sorted before you set off, you're less likely to encounter unnecessary detours, dead-ends or precipices on the way.

So even at the note-making stage there are some considerations which will help you decide what's going to be in your final book. For example, if your autobiography is to be read by others, who those readers are will help you decide what's to go in and what's to be left out. A personal memoir for your grandchildren will concentrate on the way you have lived your life, which will be so different from the way they will live theirs. It will also include information about the family of which they're a part.

A book aimed at a wider audience will have a different resonance. General readers will not be motivated to persevere through a long bundle of family information, so you will find yourself concentrating on memories that will interest and entertain. Of course, you don't have to scan through the whole of your life for these interesting episodes. You might choose to write a book that concentrates on just one period of your life which has its own special significance that would interest others, or one 'thread' that has been part of the fabric of your life. But whether you decide on a 'whole life to date' book, or a 'slice of life' book, try to choose those memories that will *inform* and/or *entertain* the general reader.

If your book is going to convey a message of some sort, your material will need to be selected with this message in mind. Some incidents might be more useful than others when it comes to illustrating your message. See Chapter 8 for the use of a message as your 'theme'.

Even if you are intending to write your memoirs as a private record of personal memories that you can look back on in later years, the looking back will be much more pleasurable if you have built some sense of order and purpose into your writing.

## Your 'First-draft' Ring-binder

Once you've got some idea of the book you're hoping to write, that is the time to start writing up your selected memories and keeping them in a specially designated file for 'book' material only.

At this stage, a ring-binder may well be more useful than yet another envelope file. It looks more like a book for one thing, which is psychologically encouraging, and the very fact that it's different helps to remind you that your envelope files are your basic 'resources', not the finished writing.

Indeed, your ring-binder won't be the finished writing either. It's a sort of halfway-house between your resources and your finished polished script. As you decide which sections of your life you want in your book, use these sections as headings on your ring-binder's card separators. Then go back to your envelope files to find the appropriate memories. *Don't just lift them out and transfer them to the ring-binder!* Some of your 'resource' notes may only be one-line notes that you know will jog your memory. When you've decided on a particular memory from one of your envelope files that you think you want to have in your book, take time to think about it and explore it, and then write it up again more fully, with as much detail as you can remember. Then put this written-up account in the appropriate section of your ring-binder.

Do remember that you are still writing notes for your ring-binder – you're not writing the book *per se*. We're still some way from that final polish, but there are some guidelines below that will help you with this intermediate writing stage.

## Writing for Your Ring-binder – First Guidelines

- *Be comfortable!* Make sure you're easy with your writing equipment. Don't try typing or word-processing if you've never done it before – unless you decide that your ring-binder writing is a good opportunity to teach yourself these skills. If you are handwriting, use the kind of pen you like best – ballpoint, rollerball, fountain pen or whatever – and stick to it. Decide whether you're going to use wide-lined or narrow-lined paper, and stick to it. If you're typing or word-processing, choose an uncomplicated font and point-size, and stick to it. Being consistent makes the job easier for you as you write your notes, easier for you as you file them and re-read them later, and easier for others if your book never gets any further than this ring-binder stage.

- *Relax!* Don't be too self-critical. These are still your intermediate notes, not the final printed book. You're not writing a school essay or doing an exam, so forget about grammar and spelling for the moment and just get those memories down! Imagine you're writing a letter to a close friend – you don't want to be formal, but you do want to get the picture across.

● *Keep on the right track!* Beware of making unnecessary detours. When you decide to write about a particular topic for a section of your ring-binder, stick to that topic and keep writing about the person, place or event as they were at that particular time in your memory. If you're suddenly reminded of something that happened later or earlier, make a quick one-line note on a separate piece of A4 to be written up and filed later in its appropriate section. But don't let pondering on the new memory interrupt the flow in writing up the one you're already working on.

● *Don't look over your shoulder!* Forget your prospective readers for the moment, whoever they might be in your imagination. Don't worry about whether they will like what you've written, or whether they will approve of it. These are your memories, this is your story. Tell it your way. (There are various tools that will improve your story later for your readers, but they are not for these ring-binder notes. See Chapter 8.)

All these guidelines are directed at getting you to write freely, easily and without inhibition. But you are not yet writing the book, only halfway-house draft notes that will be improved later. Yes, it can be frustrating not getting stuck into the final book right away! But this idea will seem less frustrating or daunting if you consider that most of the would-be autobiographies that are rejected by publishers are turned down because they are in fact just enthusiastic first drafts, not polished products. The ones that get published, bought, borrowed from libraries and enjoyed are the ones that have been carefully crafted from earlier drafts.

## Your Ring-binder Is Not the Finished Book – Further Guidelines

Successful autobiography has been described as being either the extraordinary life of an ordinary person or the ordinary life of an extraordinary person. However, there is a third possibility, and that's the ordinary life of an ordinary person, brilliantly written. Unfortunately, one can too often find examples of the worst possibility of all – the ordinary life of an ordinary person poorly written. Some of them have even found their way into print, though this is less likely since the campaign against vanity publishing has curbed the activities of unscrupulous publishers who would publish writing of any quality so long as the writer paid them (see Chapter 10).

The professional writing skills required to turn a first draft into a satisfying book are explained in Chapter 8. But it cannot be stressed too strongly at this ring-binder stage that *there are skills required*, and the budding writer who chooses to ignore this fact is courting rejection and possibly ridicule.

Many first-draft autobiographies (those that have not been carefully crafted from earlier drafts) share two characteristics. Their content is of no significance or interest to the reader and their style of writing is unnatural and inappropriate. Here are some further guidelines to help you as you write for your ring-binder.

● *Avoid insignificant content.* A national newspaper book reviewer wrote of a published 'first-draft' autobiography:

'What it screams out for is a writer to give it shape and to weed out the inconsequential. It reads as though a student rock journalist had left his tape-recorder running during an "in-depth" interview and then, instead of writing up only the nuggets of interesting information, had simply copied out everything he had been told.'

The result was a book made boring by a large part of its *content* being of no significance or interest to the reader. A shorter book that had concentrated on the 'nuggets of interesting information' would have been a better book.

Sometimes one sees chapter headings that try to make unremarkable events sound like world-shattering developments. These are often another sign of a first-draft autobiography full of insignificant detail of the kind that is signalled by a chapter title like 'I go to Stafford Street School'. You can avoid a contents page filled with such inconsequential moments by selecting from your life history only those moments that were particularly amusing, unusual, uncomfortable, triumphant, frightening, ridiculous, radiant – well, anything that is genuinely significant and engaging.

You might think that yours has been a 'Stafford Street School' sort of life, with no unusual or triumphant episodes to write about. That's not actually true. In Chapter 8 we shall see how the 'ordinary' joys and sorrows of your life can be written in such a way as to be deeply meaningful and significant to your reader.

● *Avoid unnatural and inappropriate style.* There are two main kinds of unnatural and inappropriate style that are often seen in first-draft autobiographies. First there is the 'and then' kind:

> 'and then we went to the park for the afternoon, which was very nice. Then we had tea, and then we all went to see "The Great Caruso" which was being shown twice-daily at the Odeon.'

If you think about it, this is little more than a list of activities in retrospect. Where's the interest or the entertainment for the reader?

The other kind of unnatural and inappropriate language is possibly the result of trying not to use 'and then'. Straining for 'proper' or 'good' English can result in the writer sounding very pompous, as in:

> 'The film exceeded all expectations, the purveying of a delicious assortment of ices and soft drinks during the interval being a considerable enhancement.'

This is more than a list, true, but the language is hardly the kind of language you'd use in a letter to a friend – except as a joke, perhaps. The odd line now and again might be entertaining, but as a general style it's boorish and boring.

● *Be natural.* The most satisfying autobiographies are those where the words on the page chime in the reader's mind like the natural everyday speech of the writer. The reader may not ever have heard the writer speak, of course, but if the book is written in normal, natural language, it 'sounds' like the writer speaking inside the reader's head.

The easiest way to achieve this natural language in your writing is to write as if you are penning a letter to a good friend. Not all the sentences will be absolutely correct. This one isn't. But they will 'sound' authentic, not forced. (That one isn't, either!)

It's important to get the content and style of your writing right because inconsequential content and inappropriate style just make the reader think, 'Big deal – so what? Who cares?' And they will stop reading.

Alfred Hitchcock – who knew a thing or two about story-telling – is reputed to have said that 'drama is life with the boring bits left out'. You could do a lot worse than to copy that out in large letters and stick it to the front of your ring-binder.

# 7

## YOUR AUTOBIOGRAPHY –
## CLARITY RULES

The counsel given in Chapter 6, 'forget about grammar', was obviously aimed at getting you writing freely and without inhibition. That's the best way to get your memories flowing on to the paper. But if you want to be sure that your reader understands and appreciates the whole picture you have in your mind of a particular memory, you do eventually have to play by some agreed rules of communication. Part of your polishing process will involve being aware of how your words convey your picture and how some of the rules of English grammar help them to do their job.

Take punctuation, for example – all those dots, dashes and commas that can seem an unnecessary complication when you feel it's the words that are important. Just see what can happen to words if the punctuation is missing or wrong. Take the following sentence:

The judge said the defendant was a known liar.

Now see how you can change the meaning with the deliberate addition of some punctuation:

'The judge,' said the defendant, 'was a known liar.'

Imagine you want to tell your reader that one of these two people called the other one a liar. How is your reader to know which person is making the accusation about the other? The words on their own are ambiguous. You need to use punctuation to make sure the words come across with absolute clarity in order to complete the process of effective communication.

Good writing is essentially the effective communication of the writer's thoughts and feelings to the the reader's mind via the arrangement of words on the page. If the words are arranged in a way that makes the meaning unclear or ambiguous, the reader gets a confused message.

In this chapter, we look at just a few of the ways you can confuse your reader and how to avoid them.

## The Power of the Comma

The humble comma can be very important, so treat it with respect and use it to make the words make sense. Take the sentence:

When lightning struck Richard Henry fainted.

Without a comma we don't know whether it's

When lightning struck, Richard Henry fainted.

or

When lightning struck Richard, Henry fainted.

And what a difference a comma would make to

The lion's already eaten Darren.

You can usually judge where to put a comma by reading a sentence aloud and listening for the pause, as in

The lion's already eaten, Darren.

Commas are useful for separating words that are really a little list within a sentence:

I enjoy finding books about cookery, sewing and gardening at our library.

But don't use more commas than you need to make it make sense. Don't use commas before the first item in the list or after the last item:

I enjoy finding books about, cookery, sewing and gardening, at our library.

## Some Simple Rules of Spelling

There *are* some rules to our English spelling, even in a language which confuses foreigners with *bough*, *cough*, *through* and *tough*! Here are some easy ones. They are all connected with how the words sound when you say them out loud.

● Vowels are lengthened by a letter 'e' at the end of a word. Compare *cloth* and *clothe*, *breath* and *breathe*.

● Vowels are shortened by double letters in the middle of a word. Compare *diner* and *dinner*, *hoping* and *hopping*.

● The letters 'c' and 'g' are softened to sound like 's' and 'j' only when they're followed by 'i' or 'e'. Compare *decade* and *decide*, *indefatigable* and *changeable*. This rule will help you to spell *incorrigible* correctly – *incorrigable* breaks the rule.

● Forget 'i' before 'e' except after 'c'. Yes, we all learned it as children, but you will have discovered long ago that there are too many times when it's just not true and it simply doesn't work! Instead, use the rhyme that is guaranteed to work every time:

If the sound says ee
Then the spelling's 'i – e'
Except after 'c'.

Try it – it works! Here are some examples:

*priest* (the sound says ee, so it's 'ie')
*receive* (the sound says ee, but it's after 'c' so it's 'ei')
*height* (the sound doesn't say ee so it can't be 'ie', it must be 'ei')
*weight* (the sound doesn't say ee so it can't be 'ie', it must be 'ei')
*reign* (the sound doesn't say ee so it can't be 'ie', it must be 'ei')

## My Husband and Me?

How can you tell when it's 'My husband and I' and when it should be 'My husband and me'? There are good logical reasons for using one or the other which are to do with the structure of a sentence, but here's the quick and easy way to tell – leave out the other person and just use the 'I' or 'me' and see what sounds right.

My husband and me are so pleased with the clock

would be wrong because you wouldn't say

Me am so pleased with the clock,

you'd say

> I am so pleased with the clock.

So it has to be

> My husband and I are so pleased with the clock.

But what about

> We are both so pleased with the clock you gave to my husband and I?

That has to be wrong because you wouldn't say

> We are both so pleased with the clock you gave to I.

It has to be

> We are both so pleased with the clock you gave to my husband and me.

Now you will see why 'Alice and me went to Blackpool' would be wrong.

## Inserted Phrases Can Cause Confusion

Look at this statement:

> Inflation influences voters.

There's nothing wrong there.

> Inflation and taxes influence voters

would also be correct. Sometimes you might want to use the phrase 'as well as' instead of 'and' to give more emphasis. In which case would it be

> Inflation as well as taxes influence voters

or

Inflation as well as taxes influences voters?

Influence or influences? Leave out the inserted phrase 'as well as taxes' to get the answer:

Inflation as well as taxes influences voters.

## Dangling Participles

The problem of a dangling participle is probably best explained by example. Here's a simple example:

Sighing, Alice switched off the television.

The word at the start of that sentence, 'sighing', is taken from the verb 'to sigh'. It is the present participle of the verb 'to sigh'. Because it is not firmly attached to Alice, as in 'Alice was sighing' it is a dangling participle.

Starting a sentence with an 'ing' word – a present participle like 'sighing' – can give rise to lots of confusion. There are two rules which must always be observed. They are:

1. the action of the 'ing' word must be simultaneous with the other action.
2. the action of the 'ing' word and the other action must both be done by the same person.

These two rules can be shortened to 'same time, same person.'

Check our example. 'Sighing, Alice switched off the television.' Could both these actions be done at the same time? Yes. Are both these actions done by the same person? Yes. So there is no confusion in the reader's mind with that sentence.

Here's another example which obeys both rules, 'same time, same person':

Walking around the familiar streets I met many old friends.

The walking and the meeting are logically simultaneous and it's the same person doing the walking and the meeting.

But what about this?

Running down the stairs she took her coat from behind the door.

That breaks the first rule. The two actions could not be done at the same time.

Cruising down the river, the church came into view.

That breaks the second rule. The two actions are not being done by the same person. Someone/something other than the church was presumably doing the cruising.

Not all dangling participles are 'ing' words. You can cause as much confusion with a past participle – an 'ed' word – at the beginning of a sentence. For example:

Startled by the noise, her book fell to the floor.

The 'same person' rule is broken here. It presumably wasn't the book that was startled.

The habit of starting a sentence with a dangling participle is a device that some writers (particularly beginner writers) overuse because they think it sounds rather literary. However, we rarely use it in ordinary conversation, so even if you are sure you know how to use it correctly, it may not be the appropriate style for your writing. You can nearly always convey a clear picture in direct language:

As we cruised down the river the church came into view

or

She ran down the stairs and took her coat from behind the door.

## Don't Ditch Authenticity for Grammar

Having said all that, there are occasions when (deliberate) incorrect grammar and punctuation can enhance an autobiographical work. In Chapter 8 we shall see, for example, how a character's spoken words – i.e. dialogue – have to sound authentic if the reader is to 'hear' them the way you heard them. If you were to make your war-time cockney neighbour speak with the sort of grammar we hear when the Queen opens parliament, that part of your story would be untrue. Dialogue does not have to be correct and, indeed, can be more moving, funny and believable if it is not. (See page/s 80–82 for further guidelines on writing believable dialogue.)

But there is a case, too, for not writing the main narrative of your book in absolutely correct English. Most autobiographies are written in the first person (using 'I' and 'me') which means that the reader is almost 'hearing' you speak as you write. Your story will come across as authentic and believable when the reader 'hears' your authentic voice. Any attempt to sound like someone you're not will lose you credibility with your reader. Of course, if you're the sort of person whose natural speech is always measured and grammatically correct, then your written narrative should reflect that. But most people's natural speech is more more chatty, so for most people it's not a good idea to try and write like an academic lecturer.

If sounding authentic means forgetting the grammar here and there, go for authenticity. But try to get the spelling right and make the language clear enough to get the picture across.

## The Writer's Home Library

If you're serious about your writing – and you are, or you wouldn't be reading this book – you need to think about setting up your own writer's home library, a collection of useful reference books to reach for as and when required.

Most homes have a dictionary. Make sure yours is a fairly recent one. Language evolves and changes so even dictionaries can be 'wrong' if they are too old to include new words or new meanings. For example, a pre-wireless-age dictionary would probably define 'broadcast' as something like 'scattered freely, as with seeds, not in drills or rows' without reference to radio or television. Similarly, a pre-computer-age dictionary would almost certainly define 'network' as 'system of railways, rivers etc.' and 'group of connected broadcasting stations' without reference to today's network computers, low-powered PCs that download necessary software from a central high-powered computer.

Alongside your up-to-date dictionary you should have an equally up-to-date thesaurus. A thesaurus is like a dictionary, but the words are arranged not alphabetically but according to concept. So all the words to do with, say, anger are listed together. If you want to convey how angry you felt but don't want to repeat the word 'angry' you could use your thesaurus to find words like 'furious' and 'enraged' listed with 'angry'. The index at the back of the thesaurus is in alphabetical order and refers you to the page where all the 'angry' words are listed. The word 'thesaurus' comes from the Greek word for treasure store and to a writer it is just that.

If you feel a bit hesitant about using a particular word and want to be sure you're making yourself as clear as possible, the acknowledged authority on the proper use of English is *The New Fowler's Modern English Usage* (Oxford University Press; 1996).

A very useful little all-in-one book that sorts out spelling, punctuation, grammar and jargon is the *Good Word Guide* (Bloomsbury; 1998). It lists similar words together (such as founder and flounder, curb and kerb, fewer and less) to help you choose the right one for your purpose.

The two standard handbooks for freelance writers are 'the red one' and 'the yellow one'. 'The red one' is the *Writers' & Artists' Yearbook* (A&C Black; published annually). 'The yellow one' is *The Writer's Handbook* (Macmillan; published annually). In both these handbooks you will find lists of book publishers, magazines and newspapers, agents and useful organisations. There are also helpful articles on different aspects of freelance writing.

The 'red' handbook includes a journalist's calendar so you can see in advance any significant anniversaries you might write about. It also has a list of proofreading symbols to help you correct the printer's galley proofs of your book before final printing.

The 'yellow' handbook includes comments about publishers by the authors who have been published by them – some of these are very revealing!

Always use the very latest edition, whichever handbook you choose. The world of publishing changes almost daily so last year's editors are quite likely to have moved on.

Your writer's home library should prove an invaluable 'home editor', helping you to choose and use the right words the right way to communicate your message or picture effectively to your reader.

# 8

# YOUR AUTOBIOGRAPHY –
# HOW TO MAKE IT A GOOD READ

When you come to write an autobiography you may think that the true facts as you recall them will make your story as interesting to others as it is to you, but this is not necessarily so.

Anyone who has done jury service, or even watched trial dramas on television, knows that a police report of the facts about a case is often the most boring and tedious part of the whole proceedings. The facts are of vital importance, naturally, but their importance doesn't automatically make them gripping.

Many poor first-draft autobiographies read like police reports. The reader gets all the facts, often including many unimportant facts, in a style that is either boringly monotonous or boringly pompous. The ultimate unforgivable sin for a writer is boring your reader, which is why professional writers use special techniques to make their stories gripping. Your reader doesn't want a report containing all the facts. Your reader wants a grandstand view of the action, a front-row seat for the drama, an armchair in front of the screen for the picture. Think of the books you've enjoyed yourself. The best stories – fact or fiction – are those where you feel you're right there as it's all happening.

## Ten Basic Fiction Techniques

Even if you're a complete beginner as a writer, you can write a 'couldn't-put-it-down' autobiography if you use the same techniques the professionals use. They are easy to understand and easy to apply and they 'show' rather than 'tell' the story. They are actually the ten basic techniques of fiction writing, but they can equally well be applied to factual material too.

1.  Theme
2.  Plot
3.  Characters
4.  Setting
5.  Time-span
6.  Viewpoint

7. Emotion
8. Dialogue
9. Conflict
10. Suspense

How do you portray a real-life situation which had some relevance and meaning for you in the past, in a way that will reverberate with relevance and meaning for your reader in the present? That's easy. You have to make that real-life situation seem as real to them now as it was to you then. You need to write about people who seem real, who speak, who have feelings, who react. You need to write about places that seem real, with details that make a believable picture in the reader's imagination. These ten techniques will help you.

Most fiction stories convey a theme or message, through the construction of a plot and the portrayal of characters. These characters are shown within a setting and a time-span, and the story is told from a chosen viewpoint. The reader is drawn into the action through the emotion and dialogue of the characters, and they keep turning the pages because of the conflict faced by the characters, and because of the suspense that delays answers to problems, until the final satisfying resolution.

If you use this method for your own story, it will be as good a read as any novel. We'll examine each of these techniques in turn, and then look at an example of how they enhance autobiographical writing.

## 1. *Theme*

The theme of your book is not to be confused with the plot or story-line. The theme is the idea behind the story. It can usually be described in a word like *survival*, *self-discovery*, *betrayal*, *escape*, or a phrase such as *who dares wins*, *if at first you don't succeed*, *plus ça change*. Very often it was the theme that supplied Jane Austen's titles, for example, *Pride and Prejudice*.

The theme will be the thread that runs through your story and gives it a sense of overall unity. Having a theme and being conscious of it will help you to tell your tale consistently without jumping off on to unrelated topics. Your theme will engage and entertain your readers. A strong theme, or message, will provoke or warn or encourage them.

## 2. *Plot*

The plot is the storyline, the framework on which your theme is woven. Unlike a fiction-writer, you don't have to make up your plot because you are writing about events that have actually happened. Nonetheless, your writing will be greatly enhanced if you understand the power behind a plot.

There is a school of thought which says that there are only seven original fiction plots: Cinderella (underdog gets just rewards after many ups and downs); Achilles (hero brought down by fatal flaw); Faust (the debt must be paid in the end); Tristan (the 'eternal triangle'); Circe (the inevitability of spider catching fly); Romeo and Juliet (boy-meets-girl, boy-loses-girl, possibly finds her again); Orpheus (the gift that is taken away).

It is no coincidence that these seven classic plots are known by the names of their characters. That is because all the best plots are about people working through conflicts. A glance back at those seven plots will underline this observation. And that's what gives these plots their power, their ability to grip the reader. It's the constant concern for the characters and their fate – will they, won't they? – that keeps the pages turning. At its most basic, a plot is a problem travelling towards an outcome.

Bear that in mind as you re-tell your story and you will grip your reader too.

## 3. *Characters*

The characters in your story will be you (of course!) and the real people you have encountered in your life. They are real to you who knew them; your task in your writing is to make them just as real to the reader.

A real person is not just a list of physical characteristics with a name: 'My grandfather was a tall, grey-haired man called Joe'. A real person's thoughts, words and actions reveal their actual character and personality, and these thoughts, words and actions are motivated by two things – their background (what their circumstances have made of them) and their emotions (what feelings they have towards their circumstances). If it is at all possible, you need to know your characters inside out before you write about them – their background, upbringing, schooling (because these factors will have influenced their attitudes), their prejudices, fears, ambitions (because these will affect their reactions to their circumstances and to other people).

As you write about the characters in your life, don't just *tell* the reader what they thought or said or did – think of your story almost as a stage play, and show the reader the particular character in action, revealing their personality in the things they say and do. What would he have looked like in that situation? How would he have sounded? How would he have revealed his feelings? Or would he have hidden them? And how? Did he prefer tea or coffee? Cigarettes or a pipe?

These details are important in getting the real person off the page and into the reader's mind. Your ring-binder is of great help here. Take a blank sheet of paper for each main character and put their name at the top. Then divide the page into three columns headed 'Details of appearance', 'Details of speech habits', 'Details of physical mannerisms and gestures'. Fill in the lists with as many details as you can remember and refer to them whenever you're writing about a particular character. That way you'll remember to have Grandpa Joe sniffing and muttering, 'Let's be having yer,' as he leans forward in his rocking chair to pluck his Sunday boots from behind the fender.

(The way your various characters spoke to other people and to you is also an important part of how you make your characters seem real. See 'Dialogue' below.)

Although your story may include many interesting, even colourful characters, do make sure that you are the main character. If you find yourself writing more and more about your mother (or someone else) perhaps you should be writing biography. Autobiography is your story, so stick to that.


4. *Setting*


There will doubtless be parts of your autobiography which will concentrate on places you remember from your earlier days, places that have some importance or significance in your story. In other parts, it will be the people who are more important, and the setting then becomes the 'stage-set' where the action takes place. In either case, it's the details which will paint the picture in the reader's mind.

To help you to recall and recreate these details, use the five senses as your guide – sight, touch, sound, smell and taste.

What could you see on that occasion? If your memory of a particular place is hazy on detail, do some research. Old photographs (not necessarily your own) and local history books may remind you of the way the High Street looked before the last war. A close look at walls and trees today will help you describe the walls and trees of yesterday.

What did it feel like to run a stick along the school railings? If you can't remember, go out and do it! Was it like having your teeth drilled through your wrist? An electric shock?

Did an approaching tram make a hissing noise or a shambling clang?

What were the distinctive smells in that character's house? Mothballs? Gravy? Stale beer?

What were the tastes that engraved themselves on your memory, and why? Your first encounter with fresh pineapple? Condensed milk in strong tea? Sherbet fizzing on your tongue?

Use sight, touch, sound, smell and taste to paint your stage-set for some action, or to paint a detailed picture of a special place or object that's important in your story.

## 5. Time-span

Will your story be a 'whole life to date' book, covering your lifetime? Or will it be a 'slice of life book', concentrating on one very significant period? Time-span has nothing to do with how long your book will be. You can cover several years in one chapter or take a whole book to cover one year. You have to decide which approach would be best for your theme, a whole-life-to-date book or a slice-of-life book. Only bring into your story those events which best portray your theme.

Don't worry about your reader needing to know what has happened in the past, before the main story begins. Yes, it's very tempting to want to tell the reader all the background before you get on to the main events, but it's a temptation you should resist because it delays the real start and risks boring the reader. Once you've decided which part of your life you are recounting, the reader wants to know what's happening to you at that time, not years before.

If there is information from before the start of the story which the reader at some point really does need to know, there are two ways of giving them that necessary information. You can either weave it in, as in

'the door-frames made crooked by the same war-time bomb that had demolished the laundry and robbed her of her income'.

Alternatively, it can be revealed through 'flashback'. Flashback is where the events you are describing remind you (or your character) of an earlier event, which you then 'flash back' to and tell as if it were the 'now' event. For example:

'I sat in the waiting room listlessly thumbing through a maga-zine, vaguely aware of the classical music playing in the back-ground. It was only as I realised I was counting the bars in my head that I recognised Mendelssohn's "Hebrides" overture. Once again I was at the back of the college orchestra, waiting for my entry on the timpani, sticks at the ready, one eye on the music and the other on the conductor.'

Another problem relating to time-span is the question of where exactly to begin your story. A whole-life-to-date autobiography doesn't have to start with the day you were born, unless the circumstances have some unusual significance that will kick-start the whole story. Were you born in a theatre dressing room? Or during a street party? Either way, you've got a marvellous opening! But 'I was born on the fifteenth of February 1942 in a hospital near Liverpool' is a non-starter.

It's a good idea to start your story, whole-life or slice-of-life, at a point of crisis or change. That way, your reader will immediately be interested in what has brought about the crisis or change and how you will respond to it. Choose something that will link easily with your origins if you want to go from this crisis back to the beginning in a flashback.

In this extract from a published autobiography, a new situation is the crisis or change that allows for a flashback to the beginning of the author's life. You can also see how some necessary information has been woven in.

It was my first talk to our ladies' meeting and my first talk as a vicar's wife. One of a million hurdles I'd clambered over since my husband began his training for the Church of England priesthood. He was a schoolmaster then, and we'd been married nine years already and had two small sons.

My hand was still shaking, though, as I drank the cup of tea the secretary brought me. Was maturity so much of an advan-tage, I wondered? Would I have been more or less nervous ten years younger?

A motherly lady pulled her chair alongside mine. 'That was lovely!' she said with a smile.

76

'Well, you said "tell us something about yourself,"' I answered, half apologetically.

'It took me right back, it did. In fact, I remember the day your father died. My mother met your Gran and came back to tell me the news.'

I know I smiled back at her, because I'll never forget the enormous effort it took, as the tea churned in my stomach. She remembered! There were people here who remembered more than I could. I was three years old when my father died and I have no specific recollection of the event.

'And fancy you coming back here after all these years,' she chattered on, shaking her head in disbelief. 'Fancy! And married to our new vicar! Who'd have guessed!'

Who indeed?

So much water had rushed beneath so many bridges. At what point had the river of my life set its course for this particular scene? John's ordination? Our marriage? My conversion? Or was the course set even earlier? The Methodist youth club? Childhood picnics on this very spot? Yes, maybe that was when my life began its hike towards this point.

But it could have been even earlier.

My father was killed in the last year of the Second World War, in a truck-loading accident at his army camp just two miles from home ...


6. *Viewpoint*

Most autobiographies are written from the viewpoint of the story-teller who writes in the first-person, as 'I' or 'me':

'I smiled as Mrs. Kendall slipped me a boiled sweet without my Gran seeing.'

Occasionally, an autobiography is written in the third-person, as 'he/she' or 'him/her':

'Janet would soon be ten. Already she had set her mind on going to the grammar school.'

Writing about yourself as if you were another person is perhaps a bit unusual (although Flora Thompson did this in *Lark Rise to Candle-*

*ford*) but it does have some advantages. For one thing, you might feel slightly more at ease when it comes to those skeletons in the cupboard if you're writing about yourself as if you were someone else. Similarly, you might find it easier to visualise events in your memory if you 'see' them happening to someone else.

If you stay close to your third-person main character and take care not to let the reader see or hear anything the main character cannot see or hear, you get a similar effect to first-person writing. The reader feels the emotions of the main character.

There is another viewpoint option which is considered rather old-fashioned these days. It's called the god-like or omniscient viewpoint. The writer knows and sees and recounts everything whether or not the main character is au fait with all the facts. This can have the advantage of allowing you more flexibility with suspense and plotting, because you can let your reader 'see' and 'hear' things before the main character gets to know about them.

However, unless you're a confident and experienced writer, it's perhaps better to stick with the more usual first-person viewpoint. Apart from being more natural and therefore easier, it has the enormous advantage of 'one-to-one' intimacy with the reader.


## 7. *Emotion*

Emotion is the life-force of good fiction. It gives the story life and vibrancy, and it can do the same for your autobiography. It is your characters' emotions that dictate their thoughts, words, actions and reactions, all those things which together make the plot. The emotions of the main character (you) will evoke a matching emotional response in the reader, building up an empathy which keeps the pages turning.

For all its importance, the power of emotion is often completely overlooked by first-draft autobiographers. Remember your reader – they don't want just to know what happened to you, but what it *did* to you as a person. They want to know how you *felt*. They want to see the effect your circumstances had on you. Don't cheat on them. Show them.


## 8. *Dialogue*

Real people speak directly to each other and even to themselves, so your story must contain speech, i.e. dialogue. Here are some pointers to help you write convincing dialogue.

● Dialogue is direct speech. That means instead of writing

'She told me she did not wish to go into the cowshed because it was dark',

you write

'She said, "I do not wish to go into the cowshed because it is dark."'

Direct speech is putting down the words that were actually spoken.

● Dialogue should be realistic. That means instead of writing

'She said, "I do not wish to go into the cowshed because it is dark."',

you write

'She said, "I don't want to go into the cowshed because it's dark."'

But to make it even more realistic, you might write,

'"I'm not going in that cowshed!" she insisted. "It's as black as night in there!"'

● Dialogue should be functional. That means it has a job to do, in addition to letting the reader know what words were spoken. Dialogue should do at least one of three things:

i)   reveal something about the character of the person who is speaking
ii)  pass information from one character to another and therefore to the reader
iii) instigate a response that will move the plot along.

There are two problems about writing dialogue in autobiography and they are both to do with making it realistic. You have to avoid going overboard with dialect. Trying to convey a regional accent through printed words is not easy and the result can be very hard to read. It's much better just to set the right tone in the reader's ear by using an occasional 'Ey up!' or 'Blimey!' Then ordinary English will take on

its own regional accent, as in 'Ey up! You'll not get it through gate!'
or 'Blimey! You got no chance of getting it through that gate!'

The other problem is knowing whether you're being truthful or not.
None of us can remember the exact words we, or others, spoke in
conversations years ago. Shouldn't we therefore avoid using dialogue
altogether, rather than put words in people's mouths? It depends on
what you think the truth is. It is certainly true that people did use direct
speech years ago. If you make sure that your characters never say
anything in your dialogue that would be out of character for them, and
if you recall and recreate the particular way they used to say things, then
you are giving a true picture of how a conversation would have sounded
even if it isn't a precise and accurate record of the exact words used.


## 9. Conflict

In fiction, the main character's problem is never solved immediately.
If it were, there would be no story, no chance to watch as the character
gradually finds his/her way to a solution.

In your autobiography, make your main character – you – meet
with various points of conflict on the way to the eventual 'result' at
the end of the book.

This conflict does not have to be super-dramatic if your life
hasn't been super-dramatic. Everyone faces conflict of one sort or
another almost every day of their life. Some conflict is outer conflict,
things outside yourself that slow you down, press you into new directions, even put you back a step or several steps. Some of life's
hurdles come from inner conflict, things inside yourself like insecu-
rity, indecision, fear, refusal to take things seriously, unresolved
anger.

Some first-draft autobiographers shy away from using conflict.
Their stories are all sunshine, the memories all rose-tinted. Readers
are left unsatisfied by the level blandness of these stories (readers like
to worry!) and therefore doubt their truthfulness.

Readers like to see how you have responded to conflict and will –
perhaps subconsciously – match your response with their own.


## 10. Suspense

Suspense is not the same as conflict. Suspense is keeping the reader
guessing. You can build suspense into your autobiography by not

revealing certain information to your reader at the start so that they are reading at one level to find answers for their curiosity.

Of course, readers may know from the start what the end is going to be. The outcome of your story may well be the reason for you writing the book, e.g. 'Gran's Round-The-World Balloon Trip', but it is suspense that will keep them wondering about the 'how'. How did she get into ballooning? Did she have a family? What did they think of her exploits?

Don't tell your reader too much at once. The suspense will keep them reading and enjoying your book.

Now that we have looked at each of the ten basic techniques in detail, we shall see how they can work when applied to autobiographical writing. Here is an accurate report of some facts that really happened in my own life, years ago.

> When I was a student, I was persuaded to join the college trad jazz band, although I had no experience of this kind of music. However, they needed a tuba-player and as that was my instrument I went along to one of their rehearsals. The band consisted of Mike Edwards on trumpet, Paul Thomson on clarinet, Idris Price on trombone and Jim Clifton on piano. At that stage, the band did not have a drummer. At first I was very nervous, having only played classical music on tuba, like my book of 'Twelve Russian Studies', but everyone was very friendly, and I soon realised that Traditional Jazz consists of a lot of instinctive 'busking', such as I had seen my aunt doing on the piano when I was small.

What we have here is something very like a police report. It's a list of facts about the situation, the people and the outcome. Even my nervousness is listed as a fact. The reader can't see the action or feel the emotion or warm to the characters. There's no life in this incident. All the facts are there, but none of those basic techniques that could have breathed life into them – apart from the inevitable first-person viewpoint. This account was never published.

Below is the same incident written up with the use of the ten fiction techniques to help the reader to 'see' real people developing, moving forward in a real situation. This version was published.

Encouraged by Mr. Bradshaw, the brass tutor, who decided early on that I had the makings of a fair tuba-player, I spent a lot of my time 'below stairs'. Relaxing in the peculiar solitude of a solo instrument trapped by sound-proofed walls, I worked at my 'Twelve Russian Studies', until they came to an abrupt halt one evening when the door burst open and my sanctuary was invaded by two bearded young men.

'There! I told you there was another one!'

'But she's a girl!'

'Of course she's a girl! What difference does it make? Is that or is that not a tuba?'

'Right. That is certainly a tuba.'

It was a tuba of sorts. I'd handed back the Youth Orchestra instrument to Mr Jenkins and was now learning on a college instrument that had seen better days. It was badly dented, the leaky water-key was fastened shut with knotted red string, and three of the metal stays had come adrift and had been somewhat inadequately reinforced with sticky tape.

'I'm sorry,' I said, 'is there some bother about me having this? Mr Bradshaw said I could use it as my own.'

'And you're more than welcome, I should say!'

I'd already pinned him as a Welshman before his colleague announced: 'Idris has his own wotsit, er, tuba. Trouble is, we need him to play trombone in the band.'

I hadn't seen either of these characters in the college wind band, that loud and lively siding where I'd been shunted along with all the other brass and wind players not good enough for the college orchestra.

So I asked, 'What band?'

'Why, the Jazz Band, of course!' said the Welshman. Only, the way he said it, it sounded like Jass Band. Very authentic. Early New Orleans.

'Can you play Dixieland on that thing?' demanded his friend.

'I don't know', I answered with patent honesty. 'How does it go?'

When they'd finished laughing, the Welshman looked at the first of the 'Twelve Russian Studies' and exclaimed, 'Hell, Mike! If she can get round this lot in three weeks, she won't have any trouble with "Tin Roof Blues".'

'Right, then', said Mike. 'You're in!'

'In what?'

They answered in chorus. 'The Jazz Band!'

'But I've never played jazz!' I protested.

'That's what they all say!' laughed Mike.

As they left, Idris said, 'It's a giggle, love, honest. Large practice-room, piano block, eight o'clock tomorrow night. Tata!'

It is absolutely impossible to slip unnoticed into a room whilst carrying a battered old tuba that has a propensity for dropping bits with the capriciousness of a rattle-throwing baby. My entrance was greeted with loud cheers from the rest of the band, and Idris quickly did the introductions.

'Jim Clifton on piano, Drama and English. Paul, er, Thomson wasn't it? Yes, Paul Thomson on clarinet. He's a first-year musician like yourself.' I recognised the first clarinettist from the wind band.

'Mike Edwards on trumpet you've already met, English and Art. I'm going on to trombone now you're here, but I'm really the college's other tuba-player, Idris Price. Gentlemen, this is, er, Brenda. Right?'

'Right. I hope you told them I'm new to all this?'

'The way we play, love, you could do your Russian Studies and no one would notice!'

Jim stubbed out a cigarette in the ash-tray on top of the piano. 'Still no drums, Idris?'

'There's a first-year potter who's keen, but he can't count. I felt we had to draw the line of incompetence slightly above that!'

'Right then. Let's see how we do with "Darktown Strutter's Ball" for starters.'

When Jim swung into a tinkling intro with heavy bass, a thousand memories flooded back, of family 'do's' with Aunty Kath at the piano. Then as I watched the others blend into the first chorus together, another familiarity asserted itself. I'd done this before, surely? With Marj? Yes, of course! They were busking!

Oh, they paid allegiance to a common chord progression, a 'reference' melody and Jim's authoritative left hand. But within this framework they improvised freely.

I crept in on the second chorus, and found my way through the sequence as quietly as possible. For the third and final chorus, I opened up and 'oompahed' briskly round the appropriate bass-scales with some exhilaration.

After the 'Hi-tiddly-eye-tye, brown bread!' ending, they swooped on me.

'I thought you said you couldn't play?'

'Where did you learn to do that?'

'That was no Russian Study, now. Be honest!'

It's a truism in the music world that the professionals are the professionals because they play for their living. Meaning that if you can afford to spend all your time playing your musical instrument, you're bound to get good! The improvement in my general tuba-playing during my time at Bretton Hall was in part due to the fact that I spent many hours playing it. And much of that time was with the Jazz Band. Traditional jazz became a hobby that paid dividends in agility and stamina for the Russian Studies and their like.

This time the characters – Mike Edwards, Paul Thomson, Idris Price and Jim Clifton – are not just names but real, lifelike people who speak and act and react. To add reality to the setting, the tuba is pictured as something that 'oompahs' on bass scales and has bits that tend to drop off. The reader can now see and hear it. I could have written about the instrument smelling of metal polish but that might have made the object too important in the context of the incident.

In the plotting, the lack of a drummer is conveyed through functional dialogue – in a humorous exchange between Jim and Idris.

My feelings of nervousness giving way to confidence are woven into the action through the use of words like *solitude, sanctuary, sorry, shunted, not good enough, patent honesty, impossible to slip unnoticed, I hope you told them, memories flooded back, another familiarity asserted itself, I crept in, opened up, with some exhilaration, a hobby that paid dividends.*

The extract is, in fact, from a religious autobiography published by a religious publisher, yet not only is there no mention of God, there is actually a swear word. That's because I was portraying the influence of religion on the life of a real, fairly insecure music student surrounded by a lot of real people who were both attractive and threatening. If I had used religious hindsight and written openly about being a seeker in need of God or of the other students as unbelievers with irreligious habits, the story would have been less truthful in its portrayal of the characters and certainly less interesting.

So to summarise: fiction writers 'show' events happening rather than 'tell' about them in reported account. They make their characters speak in true-to-life dialogue. They reveal their characters' personalities through their speech and through their actions and reactions. They convey mood or emotion through apt words of description threaded into the text. They keep the reader's interest through the conflict of challenge or humour. They keep the pages turning with suspense, the skilful weaving in of problems and solutions. Yes, fiction techniques all of them. But these techniques can make your autobiography a really good read.

# 9

## ALTERNATIVE AUTOBIOGRAPHIES

Use a little lateral thinking, and you will be able to produce an autobiography which is not simply yours because it tells your story, but also because the medium through which the story is told is unique and captivating.

The 'non-standard' autobiography is usually written for its author, and family and friends. Why not do your own thing, and make it a book none of them will ever forget? And you may find that its original format has a commercial outlet after all.

This chapter outlines four possible approaches to 'different' styles of autobiography, covering a life discovered in poetry, a multi-format autobiography, a 'life of the family' style collection, which includes material by other people related to you, and a 'compilation' book, where you put your own reminiscences beside those of others who shared specific experiences.

These are just a few examples. They are offered as starting-points from which you can experiment, always remembering that you could decide to ignore all the techniques offered and adopt something completely different in order to write your definitive book in the way you want to write it.

### Your Life in Poetry

If you enjoy poetry, whether you're experienced in writing it or not, you may like to tell your story in the form of a sequence of individual poems, or in a single, long screed. (Have a look at Wordsworth's *The Prelude* to see how effective this latter technique can be.) When choosing between these styles, consider any poems you have written in the past. If you have tried a few different forms and enjoyed experimenting with them, the first alternative is likely to be your choice. If you are not at all experienced, you could write a long piece in one simple form, to save having to learn lots of technical devices before you put creative pen to paper.

The autobiographical sequence consists of a number of separate poems, each of which stands on its own, but which can be put together to show a more complete picture. If this is to be your approach, it's a good idea to start planning the project by highlighting certain times in your life which would make good subjects for poems.

Assuming that you are going to write chronologically, a list of 'milestones' might read like this:

- First conscious memory
- Pre-school days
- Starting school
- Family Christmas
- Great-grandma
- Learning to ride a bicycle
- Childhood holidays
- First bereavement
- Winning the long jump award
- First love

Naturally, everyone's milestones will be different and will span different periods of time. The outline suggested here might cover ages four to fourteen. It helps to have rough parameters in mind even before you start to write. Intending to write about random details from ten years of your life is far less daunting than attempting the whole spread from birth to the present day.

You might prefer to take a more detailed look at varied aspects of your life at one particular time. For example, you could focus on the year you came of age, or married, or moved from primary to secondary school. Your starting-points would move laterally from one thing to another, rather than chronologically. A list of ideas based on your life at the age of twelve, for example, might include:

- Best friends
- Our house
- Parents' car, and how I used to wash it to make pocket money
- The football match
- Visits to my cousins
- My favourite book
- Cinema trips
- Being 'dared' to commit some act of petty crime
- School speech day
- Chicken pox

Having identified the subjects for your sequence of poems, you might find it useful to expand each brief heading into a series of notes. Your collection of notes on any given subject may seem dull and ordinary. If that is the case, you may decide to drop that subject from your list of ideas. Suspend the subject, though, rather than rejecting it completely. The uninspiring ideas of today may take wing and become the stunning work of tomorrow.

The exciting part is where your imagination and memories take off, and start to surprise you with their associated ideas and recollections. If you find yourself scribbling furiously, scarcely thinking about what you are putting down – don't stop. The thought/idea/ Muse has gripped you, and you should follow it as far as it is willing to take you.

When you have completed a number of sets of notes, and feel that the sequence is beginning to take shape in your imagination, it's time to start producing the actual poems.

Each separate poem you write demands to be written in a certain way. Don't feel that your first attempt to set the poem on paper is sacrosanct. Be willing to experiment, and to look at your work critically to decide whether it is emerging in the best form or not.

Here are a few ideas for simple forms. If you're not accustomed to writing in set forms, try these three easy ones first. If they are successful and you enjoy them, experiment further. (The dynamics of the different forms will be found in any good book specialising in the production of poetry.) If they do not work for you, look at the next section on free verse. In each case an example has been offered, dealing with the same subject of a first day at school.

● *Ballad stanza.* As its name suggests, this is a good pattern to use when telling a story. There are just four lines in each stanza, the first and third consisting of four measures (or 'feet') and the second and fourth of six measures. The second and fourth lines rhyme. You may repeat this quatrain (four-line stanza) as many times as you wish to communicate a complete anecdote or message. E.g.:

The yard was full of boys and girls
Who chased and laughed and played.
I held my Mum's hand tight to show
That I was not afraid.

● *Haiku.* This is a Japanese syllabic poem, where the true poetry is perceived through the medium of a syllable count. Haiku may be untitled, and they do not rhyme. They have just three lines, with a pattern of five syllables in the first line, seven in the second and five in the third. The best examples of this form are 'open-ended', allowing the reader to speculate that there could be more to come. A haiku is complete in itself, but any number of them may be grouped together as stanzas of a longer poem. Traditionally, haiku include some reference to the natural world, and some to the time or season in which the poem is set. For example:

Summer done, and school
beckoned with its teachers, boys,
conkers and knowledge.

- *Triolet.* This form is just eight lines long, and uses only two rhymes. The first and second lines are repeated at the end, and the first line also recurs as the fourth. The third and fifth lines rhyme with the first, fourth and seventh, and the sixth line rhymes with the second and eighth. Lines may be of any single length, and generally use the same metrical pattern, with its regular repeated occurrences of stressed and unstressed syllables. Tiny variations in the wording of repeated lines are acceptable. Alterations to the grammar and/or punctuation are encouraged. E.g.:

I had to leave my mother's side
to learn new lessons every day.
The yard was noisy, busy, wide.
I had to leave my mother's side –
I bit my lip, but never cried,
not even when she walked away.
I had to leave my mother's side
to learn new lessons. Every day.

- *Free verse*, which does not rely on chiming rhyme sounds or a series of metrical stresses to convey its message, is a fascinating challenge. Here you have no pre-set boundaries. You must, however, be sure that you are producing free verse rather than merely chopping up paragraphs of prose and putting them on separate lines. An appreciation of the distinction tends to be instinctive. But you can hone the instinct by reading good free verse in collections and literary magazines, absorbing the most effective styles and judging your own work by their standards.

You can write as few or as many lines as you wish, in a solid block or split into separate stanzas where you choose to divide them. Lines don't have to be of a set length – but do remember that the final word in a line holds a tiny additional stress, even if there is no punctuation at the line end, and the sense of what you are saying continues into the next line. Don't squander this valuable line-end point by using a weak or insignificant word there, such as 'in' or 'a'.

Because of its lack of 'rules', free verse needs to be subjected to a rigorous revision process, to ensure that you are using the medium powerfully and appropriately.

Taking the same theme as before, a free verse poem about the first day at school might read something like this:

I squeeze Mum's hand,
see bigger children running giddy
in games I do not know.
We walk between them where
an empty mouth of corridor gapes
and at its door
a lady waits and smiles.

Mum kisses me,
pushes me forward. I can still feel
where her fingers held my hand.

Although free verse does not use full rhyme, it is enhanced by the inclusion of 'slant' rhyme, where similarity of sound provides a resonant touch. Note the similarity in a few examples of slant rhyme shown here: bigger/giddy; games/gapes/lady/waits; corridor/door; still/feel. A single example of slant rhyme, or sound similarity, would pass unnoticed, as a mere quirk of the pronunciation of the language. Use plenty of examples throughout the poem (not just at line ends,) and their poetic message is reinforced.

Some writers prefer a sequence of poems all written in the same form. Others take a more flexible approach (which is, I believe, more interesting to read) and use a variety of patterns. In a sequence, it is customary to give each poem its own title, or to number the separate poems.

Earlier in this chapter, I mentioned the possibility of writing about a time of your life in a single, long poem. For ease of reading, it would be a good idea to break the poem down into shorter sections divided by white space. There is no need to find a new title for each section, or to number them. The single 'blanket' title of the work is enough.

Probably the best form to use for this type of poem is blank verse, the name given to any number of lines written in unrhymed iambic pentameter. It takes a little practice to get into the 'way' of writing in this pattern – but the more you do it, the more naturally it occurs, and in no time you will be skimming through your material effortlessly.

A single line of iambic pentameter has ten syllables, i.e. five feet, each consisting of an unstressed syllable followed by a stressed one. This example, using the same theme as before, illustrates the pattern.

> We walked into the schoolyard, holding hands,
> and I was frightened of the children who
> all looked much bigger, braver than I was.
> The teacher waited in a doorway where
> a corridor stretched dark into my future,*
> and as I walked with her, my fingers still
> felt warm from Mum's. I tried hard not to cry.

Particularly in a long poem, absolutely unvaried metre would become tedious to read. An occasional extra unstressed syllable at the end of a line (feminine ending, example marked *) or the occasional substitution of a different metrical foot (e.g. a trochee, where the foot stress pattern is reversed to offer a stressed syllable followed by an unstressed one) adds pleasing variety. Remember, there is a big difference between a variant of the usual format to make the piece sound more interesting, and a line which uses the wrong metre because you couldn't get it right!

If you would like further information on any aspect of poetry, consult *The Craft of Writing Poetry* by Alison Chisholm (Allison and Busby; 1992).


## A Multi-Format Autobiography

If you're writing a book, the assumption is that you will be using the same medium throughout, but you don't necessarily have to produce your life story like this. Different parts of your life are recalled in different ways, so why not reflect this by merging a number of styles of writing? By writing the book in this way, you will come to each area of it with a fresh approach, which will animate the whole project.

If you have written any aspects of your life story in the form of humorous or nostalgic articles, anecdotal letters, poems or fiction-alised accounts, these could be included. Why not incorporate some of these approaches as well?

- A day-by-day account, diary style, of a short but intense period, such as the course of an illness or a special holiday. It should be easy and conversational in tone, and may read something like this:

SATURDAY
I have never flown before, so the adventure started with the airport. I couldn't believe how large the planes looked on the ground. Now that I'm up in one, it feels quite small and cramped, and I'm very sorry for the stewards dashing back and forth with trolleys of food, drinks, perfume for sale and so on ...

SUNDAY
The hotel is brilliant, but the town itself is grotty. I'm sitting on the balcony, and from here I can see a rat foraging in the gutter just beyond the gates. If it puts so much as a whisker through the gateway, I'm off to complain to the rep ... etc.

- A similar diary format covering a longer period, examining random dates rather than offering a piece for every day. Don't agonise over timing this if you have no diary information contemporary with the events you are describing. The actual, true date is less important than a general feel for the passage of time, so the dates can be manufactured.

- A short piece may be written in dialogue, just as if you were writing a scene from a play. You could even intersperse the dialogue with short bridging passages, e.g.:

MUM You can forget about going out this evening unless you've tidied your bedroom first.
SELF But I'm the one who lives in it. And I like it as it is.
MUM Like it? It's a positive health hazard! And it may be your room, but it's my house. Now get started on it. I'll come back upstairs in half an hour, and if you haven't finished ...
SELF I know, I know. You won't let me out. It's like living in a bloody prison.
MUM How dare you swear at me! I'll tell you what, my girl ...
SELF I only said 'bloody'.
MUM And if you say it again you're grounded for a week. Your Dad and I don't swear, and I'm not going to put up with it from you.

Conversations like this were commonplace when I was thirteen or fourteen. Mum had a point. I was the untidiest creature on earth (I still am, but now I'm married to a man who is equally untidy). Mum tried every way she could to make me tidy up. She'd threaten, plead, cajole, bribe – but the room remained a mess. Sometimes she piled jeans, shoes, mascara, school books etc. onto the bed, so I would have to move them before I went to sleep. Then I'd put them all back on the floor.

On the few occasions when I did blitz the problem, another conversation inevitably arose.

SELF Mum, I can't find my homework.
MUM Are you sure you've done it?
SELF Yes, of course I have. I put the book under the bed. Have you moved it?
MUM No. Why was it under the bed?
SELF Because there wasn't enough room in the middle of the floor ...

The sentence in parentheses in the bridging passage takes the reader out of the immediate situation by updating the information. This technique may work well, but can spoil the flow of the writing. If you incorporate it, apply it carefully to make sure it is used appropriately.

● Letter format. Why not describe some of the events you wish to include as if you were telling them in a letter to an imaginary friend? You could make it more realistic by manufacturing a complete relationship with the 'friend,' e.g.:

10th July, 1971
Dear William
Just a quick note to thank you for calling on us last week. Sorry we missed you, we'd only gone out for a bit of shopping. I hope your father's feeling better now – you must be exhausted, having to run about after him all the time.

Anyway, another reason why I was sorry to miss you is that I really wanted to tell you about all the trouble we had with the car. We were just driving through Thirsk, minding our own business, when a lorry swung right across the road and smashed into us. I was covered with glass, and shaking all over, but fortunately neither of us was seriously hurt. The silly thing was, I'd taken my test the previous day, and failed it. I didn't even want to drive, but I was feeling so fed up about failing I'd said I was never going to drive again ...

The preamble offers a brief touch of realism before you reach the 'meat' of the piece – the information you want to convey about your life story.

Not only can you vary the techniques of writing in this type of book, but if you're writing it as a 'one-off' purely for the interest of yourself and a limited circle of readers, you can introduce other items. School reports, concert programmes, press cuttings, bus tickets, post-cards, photographs, birthday cards, certificates etc. can be exhibited among the pieces of writing.

If you are including these things, you will need to decide on the best manner of presenting the collection. You could produce your life story scrapbook style, with your writings stuck into a book along with the mementoes. Or you might buy a loose-leaf file and fill it with plastic slip covers, into which you can insert either your typed pages or the memorabilia.

The main thing to remember is that the story is yours – and you must be totally happy with the way it is written and displayed.

## The Family's Life

Another method of producing a book about your life is to incorporate information from those people who have shared it. You will need their co-operation from the outset. You could ask the members of your family to write their own life stories, but requesting such a huge commitment would be trespassing too heavily on even the kindest of relatives.

It would be more realistic to ask each person to provide informa-tion about a single, specific time or event. For example, you might ask each member of the family to say where they were and what they were doing on the day the youngest child was born, and then create a composite picture of that day. Or you could ask them all to select a time of their own choosing which has a special significance for them, and to write a detailed account of that.

A pooling of photographs and memorabilia could be arranged, and a family archive would result which would delight generations to come.

If you are going to ask other members of the family to contribute to a book, it is important to lay down some ground rules. Decide whether you want everybody to write an account – essay style – of

their memories for you to edit and write up in your own words; or
whether they will all be asked to produce material in a form of their
own choosing for incorporation in the book just as they have
presented it.

Anyone who is not keen on writing should be encouraged to speak
their memories into a sound recorder, which you will be able to write
up at your leisure. If there is any reluctance to record, why not devise
an 'interview' to guide the subject through the information you are
seeking? Have enough questions planned to elicit all the details you
need, and be prepared to amend the list of questions while you work.
You may find that the reluctant speaker will warm up to the task, and
provide you with masses of material you hadn't even asked for. This
is a bonus. Encourage your subject to talk about anything and everything, and you will reap a richer harvest than you were expecting by
exploring all the digressions.

If the thought of doing this sounds too formal, try to get two or
three people together and suggest that they switch on the machine and
then simply have a chat, focusing their conversation on the areas you
require. One of my most treasured possessions is a tape of my parents
discussing Christmas in Liverpool during the nineteen-thirties and –
forties. It is interspersed with teatime business, such as 'Ready for
another cup?' and 'Could you pass the sugar?' As mechanical failures
can happen, it's useful to keep backup copies of material of this
nature.

There is an added bonus to this method of contributing information. You will be able to build up a sound archive to complement the
written work – again, a fascinating gift for future generations.

## Compilation Books

The family archive idea is taken a step further when you produce a
collection of writing from a large group of people who have shared a
particular experience. For example, why not contact everyone you
can find who attended school with you? Fellow pupils, teachers and
parents will all have their tale to tell. Draw them out along the lines
you intend by asking them to focus their memories, perhaps on discipline within the school, homework policy, sports day, etc.

Or get in touch with everyone you can who lived in your road in
a certain year. Ask them to send you their memories and impressions,
and even, perhaps, their feelings about the neighbours (as long as they
are printable). Again, it is useful to jog the memories by leading

contributors into specific areas of thought. Ask them to recall the local shops they used, their postman or window cleaner, any skirmishes with the local authority.

When you collate all the material you receive, don't forget to include your own responses as well. You can become so wrapped up in other people's work that you accidentally shelve your own.

Material of this kind can provide a useful underpinning of the book about your life at that time, but it has an extra value. With the agreement of the contributors (gained in case it's required, at the time of soliciting their information), collate all the memories for inclusion in a self-published book or booklet. This could be sold to raise funds for causes reflected in its content.

As with the family collaboration, be willing to accept spoken memories on tape, or to interview people to aid their flow of memory.

Any of these ideas is fun to organise and fascinating to compile. And because memory is such a haphazard device, at any moment you could think up or be presented with an amazing 'aside' which could fuel your next book.

# 10

# GETTING YOUR BOOK INTO PRINT

You are now in no doubt at all that your life experience is a unique and abundant resource for many genres of writing. Thanks to the information in this book you know how to use your reminiscences as the basis for readers' letters, articles, stories and poems. But perhaps the most popular ambition amongst those who wish to see their memories in print is to see their completed life-story in the form of a published book. That's a very understandable ambition. The moment when you first hold a new, shiny, commercially printed and bound book which you have written yourself is a moment of unsurpassable joy.

Before we get carried away on a wave of euphoria, let's spend some time thinking about the process that comes between the writer's desk and the bookseller's shelf.

Before you send your written story to a publisher it needs to be put into an appropriate form for a publisher to read. And you'll have to decide which publisher you will send it to. You will only send sample extracts at first, but these have to be accompanied by a synopsis and a covering letter. If you're lucky enough to get your story accepted, there will be a contract to sift through. You will usually receive part of the money that forms your 'advance' at this stage. Further payments will come with your completion of the manuscript and again with the actual publication of the book. Details about royalty payments will be in the contract.

To make your book as good as it can be, the publisher will quite possibly want you to make some changes and even then, the publisher will usually want to edit it further in places. Months into the process you'll have to check the proofs. Meanwhile, the publisher's sales and marketing team will be preparing extracts and dummy covers to show to the booksellers to persuade them to place their orders. There's a long journey to be travelled between the end of the writing and the start of the shelf-life.

## Preparing Your Book Manuscript for a Publisher

The first step in that journey is the preparation of the manuscript. Here are some guidelines to help you.

• Your manuscript must be typed or printed off from a word-processor. Today's busy editors don't have time to read handwriting. If you're not able to type your work yourself, ask round the family or watch the small ads in your local shops and newspapers. Lots of people will do excellent typescripts for a modest charge.

• Use plain white A4 paper and type on one side only. If you're using a typewriter, make sure you use a good black ribbon.

• Your writing must be 'double-spaced', i.e. have two line-spaces between each line of type. For normal pages, leave a 40mm (1.5 in.) margin down the left side of the paper, and leave 25mm (1 in.) down the right and at the top and bottom. Don't be tempted to 'justify' to the right (i.e. make the right-hand ends of all the lines into a neat right-hand edge like the left edge of type). Editors don't like this. Indent new paragraphs but don't leave extra line spaces between paragraphs. And it's now more common to leave only one space after a full-stop, not two.

• Make your first page a 'cover sheet'. Type your name and address in the top right-hand corner. Type the title of your book 120mm (5 in.) down the page in the centre, in capital letters. Don't underline your title – underlining tells the printer you want something to appear in italics in the final version. Under the title type 'by', in lower case, and under this type the name you wish to appear as the author of the book. This could be a pseudonym if you wish. The cheque will be sent to the name at the top of the page, which of course will be the name on the contract. Your cover sheet should not have a page number.

• On the first page of each chapter, type the name and/or number of the chapter at the top left. Number your pages consecutively through the whole book - don't start new numbers for each chapter.

• Always keep a copy of everything you send to a publisher. If you write on a word-processor or computer, back up (copy) your work on to a floppy disk regularly, in case of computer failure.

• Complete book manuscripts should be packed without clips or fastenings in an A4 box or an envelope-type folder. In the first instance however, only send a synopsis, and two chapters. Each of these should be fastened with a paper-clip in the top left-hand corner.

● Don't fold your pages. Send them in an envelope big enough to keep them flat. Enclose a stamped addressed envelope for the possible return of your proposal etc., or adequate stamps for the return of your boxed complete manuscript.

## Finding the Right Publisher

When you've spent a long time writing a whole book and you're eager to see it appear in print, taking the trouble to 'target' it at the most appropriate publisher can seem like a waste of precious time. Surely any publisher will do?

The answer to that is a definite 'no', simply because not all publishers deal with all kinds of books. Many manuscripts get rejected out of hand just because they cover a topic the publisher never publishes. How do you find out which publishers produce what is known as 'light autobiography'? There are two ways of finding out and you should use both. The first is the 'hands-on' method, and the second is the 'handbook' method.

For the 'hands-on' method, go to the largest bookshop you can get to and ask where they shelve the autobiographics. Do some careful browsing until you find the books which are closest to what you think your book is going to be like. Then you can check which publisher is doing that kind of book at the moment. You'll find the publisher's details a couple of pages in from the front cover.

It's important to note what length of book each publisher deals with – they do vary. You need to know their preferred length so that you can tailor your book to match their requirements. Book lengths are measured by the approximate number of words in the book. Book lengths are not always governed by artistic balance and structure. It's usually to do with how the publisher's preferred print size fits on pages cut in multiples of sixteen from the printer's huge sheets of paper.

To find the length of a printed book, turn to a typical page, count a few lines to find the average number of words per line. Multiply this by the number of lines on the page to get the approximate number of words on an average page. Then multiply by the number of pages to find the total word count for the whole book. Don't include title pages and the technical information at the beginning of the book.

You can use this same method to work out the number of words in your completed manuscript if your word-processor doesn't have a word-count facility.

You should come out of the bookseller's after this 'hands-on' research with a list of possible publishers and their preferred lengths. Don't try to do this research in your public library. The books there will not necessarily be typical of their publishers' current output. Publishers do change the topics they publish from time to time.

After you've done your 'hands-on' research to discover which publishers are the likely ones for your book, you then move on to method two, 'handbook' research. Check out the entries for these publishers in the latest editions of the excellent handbooks for writers mentioned in Chapter 7 – the *Writers' & Artists' Yearbook* and *The Writer's Handbook*. You can do this checking in your library if they have the very latest editions of the handbooks, but please don't rely on an out-of-date edition as things change so rapidly in publishing that the information given will almost certainly be wrong.

The reason for doing all this research is twofold. First, it's the way to find out which publishers are doing your kind of book. But just as important, it's the way to find out what these publishers want from you. You'll stand a much better chance of getting a publisher to look at your work if you tailor it as closely as possible to that publisher's current norm.

Sometimes a writer will think that if his or her book is really good, the publisher will be glad to publish it just the way it is. Sadly, that's not true. Publishers are looking for books which will fit in with their established policy and budgeted forward planning – they will not change the character of their projected list to accommodate your book.

There is no reason why you shouldn't target more than one publisher at a time, but as soon as you have a definite acceptance from one it's courteous to inform the others that the book is no longer being offered.

## Vanity Publishing

You may have seen advertisements in some magazines and newspapers which invite authors and/or poets to send in their manuscripts. They say something like 'Let us publish your book' or 'Poems wanted for new anthology'.

At first sight you get the impression that there's really no need to spend time and energy in research, looking for the best publisher for your work – there are publishers out there who are so keen to get their hands on your manuscript that they put advertisements where you will see them!

In fact, there are now not so many advertisements of this kind as there once were. And some magazines and newspapers print warnings about sending your manuscript to publishers who advertise in this way.

That's because there has been a campaign in recent years against some unscrupulous organisations and individuals who have exploited the writer's natural desire to see their work in print. They are known as 'vanity publishers' because they exploit the writer's vanity. But what their advertisements never hint at is the fact that instead of them paying you, you will have to pay them.

The accepted definition of a vanity publisher is 'any person or company charging a client to publish a book or offering to include short stories, poems or other literary or artistic material in an anthology, and then inviting those included in it to buy a copy of that anthology'.

How much do vanity publishers charge? In 1997, BBC Radio 4's investigative programme 'Face the Facts' featured some writers who had paid vanity publishers sums ranging from £2,800 to £14,400 in the hope of having their books published. Other vanity publishers produce poetry anthologies containing single poems by over 1500 different contributors, then offer the finished anthology to all the contributors at between £50 and £70 a copy.

There is absolutely no law against paying someone to publish your work for you. You may decide that this is a convenient way to get your work into print. But before you approach a vanity publisher you must ask yourself two questions. What are you getting for your money? What exactly does the vanity publisher do with the money you hand over?

Some of your money goes to pay someone to typeset your words ready for printing. Some of it goes to buy a design for the cover. Some of it goes to the printer. Some of it goes to the bookbinder. (Incidentally, it is quite usual for vanity publishers not to have all the printed pages bound into books, but have them bound piecemeal as and when people order copies.) Very little, frequently none, of your money goes in sending books or samples to the usual high street booksellers, or to pay for advertising, or in any kind of marketing. Most of your money goes to, and stays with, the vanity publisher.

Do these publishers edit your work so that it is as good as it can be? No. Regular publishers edit your work because they want it to be good enough for booksellers to buy it. They need booksellers to buy it and sell it on in great numbers so that they can recoup all the money they've laid out on editors, graphic artists, printers, distributors – and on you, the writer.

The vanity publisher doesn't need your book to be good because it doesn't matter if it doesn't sell as the publisher has not risked money on it. On the contrary, the publisher has made money from it. It is usual for a vanity publisher to print whatever is submitted. While your own work might be brilliant, you could find it on the same mail order list, or on the same page in an anthology, as pathetically poor work.

The writer receives the contracted number of 'free' copies (which, when you think about it, s/he has in fact already paid for) and after that must purchase further copies from the publisher. Other purchasers of your book may include local shops if your book has local interest, or specialist societies of your book has something special to say to them. But regular booksellers rarely, if ever, order from vanity publishers. They know that the contents will be unedited and possibly poorly written and often the printing and binding is of poor quality too. So overall sales of a vanity published book are generally very low. It would be most unusual for a writer to recoup the outlay.

## Self-Publishing

Where you could, and should, recoup the outlay of paying to have your book published is in self-publishing. This is where the writer undertakes to do everything the publisher would normally do. The writer decides to find their own printer and bookbinder and then pays them direct to produce some copies of their book. The printer will usually arrange type-setting and design, too. This is a very much cheaper option than going to a vanity publisher because there is no vanity publisher's cut.

However, you are still left with the same gaps in the process if you don't use a regular publisher. Who is going to edit your work to make it as good as it can be? It really is worthwhile getting someone who knows about these things to have a look at it. There are writers' magazines which carry small ads from editorial consultants. A local writers' group might also be helpful.

And after your books are printed and sitting in boxes or brown paper parcels in your garage, who is going to market them and distribute them? If you know you have a ready market or a good relationship with all your local bookshops, self-publishing is certainly worth considering. You probably won't make a lot of profit, but if the cover price is sensible you needn't make a loss.

## Desktop Publishing

Desktop publishing is a kind of self-publishing, only instead of having your book commercially typeset, printed and bound by the local printers and bookbinders, you find someone who can prepare the pages on computer and print them and copy them on a fast litho printer or copier. It's a bit like high-class photocopying.

Computer software for page-setting is so widespread and sophisticated these days that desktop publishing (DTP) is something of a home-industry. With the addition of a comb-binding machine, a very basic office can produce impressive-looking books very cheaply. There's the added advantage of being able to order small print-runs, which are no inconvenience to the desk-top publisher.

But once again, watch those gaps – editing and marketing! Make sure your work is thoroughly and sensitively edited and don't purchase more copies than you can get rid of.

## What to Send to the Publisher

There are many advantages to having your book published by a regular publisher. Your work is edited up to selling standard, there is no cost to you, indeed you get paid an advance and royalties, your books go on sale all over the country and if they're borrowed from public libraries you also get further payment in the form of a Public Lending Right fee. (PLR is dealt with later in this chapter.)

When you have identified the regular publishers who are likely to be interested in your kind of book, you should prepare a package to send to them. This should consist of a book proposal, a synopsis of the book's contents, two sample chapters and a covering letter.

Your book proposal is actually an assessment of the book's objectives. Do you know what your book's objectives are? What will the reader get from reading your book? Does it have a theme? In your assessment of your book's objectives you are actually 'selling' the idea of your book to the publisher. Just saying that it's your life story (or part of it) is not enough. You must say something about what has made that story worth recording and worth passing on.

The synopsis of a book is like an expanded list of contents. You list all the chapters, saying in note form what are the key events or ideas that will appear in each one. If you are planning to include photographs or drawings in your book, you should also say what your intentions are with regard to relevant illustrations.

Your two sample chapters should be the first chapter and another from some way into the book. Because there can only ever be one opening chapter, including a later chapter gives the publisher two very different samples that will show off your wide capabilities.

With your proposal, synopsis and sample chapters you will also need to send a covering letter. This should be addressed to the publisher (or publisher's editor) by name if at all possible. These are sometimes included in the information given in the writers' hand-books, but you can always phone a publishing company and ask for the name of the person who deals with autobiography. Keep the letter short and to the point – you enclose a proposal and synopsis for a light autobiography, with two sample chapters, which you hope they will consider. Enclose a stamped addressed envelope for their reply, large enough for the return of the whole package if necessary.

## Public Lending Right

If your book is likely to be stocked by public libraries you should apply to be listed on the register for Public Lending Right payments. You will find all the details in the writers' handbooks, but basically what happens is this:

For a book to be eligible it must be printed, bound, have an ISBN number and be available for purchase. Vanity-published and self-published books can be registered if they meet these requirements. There is no charge for getting on the PLR register.

Every year, a sample of library book loans is taken from a large number of selected libraries all over the UK. (The sample libraries are changed each year.) The number of loans for each book borrowed is then multiplied in proportion to the overall total of library borrowing to give a figure for the probable number of times a single book has been issued on loan across the UK in the year.

Payments are made annually to the registered authors of the borrowed books at a rate of between 2p and 3p per loan for each of their registered titles. It might not sound much, but it's a welcome extra on top of your advance and royalties. Perhaps even more important, it's a reminder that someone somewhere has gone into their library, taken your book from the shelf, flicked through the pages and not just liked what they've seen, but liked it enough to take *your book* home to read and enjoy.

So start writing now!